ROSE PETAL WINE

Also by Vasyl Symonenko in English:

"**Ballad About a Stranger**," "**The Court**," "**Ode to a Corn Cob which Died at the Supply Depot**," "**Thief**," "**I Flee from Myself...**," "**Choir of the Elders**" from the Poem "Fiction," "**To Parrots**," "**Monarchs**" and "**The Prophecy of 1917**." In *Four Ukrainian Poets: Drach, Korotych, Kostenko, Symonenko*. Trans. Martha Bohachevsky-Chomiak and Danylo S. Struk. Ed. with an Introduction by George S. N. Luckyj. [Toronto]: Quixote, 1969.

Hranitni obelisky Granite Obelisks: Selected Poetry. Trans. Andriy M. Freishyn-Chirovsky. [Jersey City, NJ]: Svoboda, 1975.

Silence and Thunder: The Selected Poetry of Vasyl Symonenko. Trans. Michael M. Naydan. Lviv: Piramida, 2017.

"**Grantite Obelisks, Like Medusas...**," "**In My Soul...**," "**Everything Was There...**" and "**The People Are Beautiful...**," trans. Michael M. Naydan, and "**The Ukrainian Lion**," trans. Vera Rich. In *A Hundred Years of Youth: A Bilingual Anthology of 20th Century Ukrainian Poetry*. Ed. Olha Luchuk and Michael M. Naydan. Lviv: Litopys, 2000.

Vasyl Symonenko

ROSE PETAL WINE

Translated from the Ukrainian
by Yuri Tkacz

Bayda Books
Melbourne 2022

First published in Australia in 2020.
This edition 2022.

Bayda Books
P.O. Box 178,
East Brunswick, 3057, Australia

FICTION
ISBN 978 0 908480 48 7

Contents

Foreword...7
Rose Petal Wine...10
Roosters Crowed on the Sashes.................................14
The Black Horseshoe...18
He Stopped Her from Sleeping..................................20
Opanas Krokva's Wedding.......................................23
A Ballad About Grandpa..25
The Incredible Interview..30
Smiles Never Offend Anyone....................................33
The Grey Package...36
The Psychological Joust...39
White Apparitions...42
A Banquet in the Threshing Yard...............................46
A Naïve Young Girl..50
Odium..54
The One-Armed Forester...77
Balm..83
A Friend of the Family..85
A Conversation Overheard.......................................87
No One Knows...89
My Student Years...92
Scraps of Thoughts...97

Foreword

Vasyl Symonenko was born on 8 January 1935 in the village of Biyivtsi, Lubny District, Poltava Province into the family of a collective farmer.

His mother, Hanna Fedorivna Shcherban, worked on the collective farm from the day of its inception until the autumn of 1957. His father, Andriy Leontovych Symonenko, a soldier, abandoned the family before young Vasyl was a year old.

During the years of German occupation, the young Symonenko lived with his mother on occupied territory. He was six to seven years old then.

In 1942 he started grade one at Biyivtsi Primary School. After finishing four grades at this school, he studied for a year at the Yenkivtsi Seven-Grade School, and then transferred to the Tarandyntsi Middle School, from which he matriculated in the summer of 1952 with a gold medal. At this school he took part in the voluntary Association for Assistance to the Army, Navy and Air Force, and also participated in sporting, mathematical and literary circles. While at school he wanted to be a war correspondent.

In 1952 he was accepted into the faculty of journalism at the Kyiv State University, from which he graduated in July 1957. Later that year he began work in the culture department of the newspaper *Cherkas'ka Pravda*.

He married Liudmyla Pivtoradnia in the spring of 1957, and in 1958 she bore him a son, Oles. His wife worked as a controller at a chemical plant and his mother lived with them.

In 1960 he became a department head at the newspaper *Molod' Cherkashchyny*, and in 1963 transferred to *Robitnycha hazeta* as their regional journalist so that he could spend more time in rural areas, which he loved. Though principally a poet, he also wrote prose and literary criticism.

Symonenko died in Cherkasy on 14 December 1963 at the early age of twenty-nine. He had been writing for only ten years. But in this time, he was able to say more than most people were able to express in a lifetime.

Even after his death, interest in his works continued to grow. This was aided by circulating accounts of dramatical episodes from his life: his clashes with the Party bureaucracy, his connections with the dissidents Ivan Dziuba and Ivan Svitlychny, and the controversial details surrounding his final illness and death.

Upset by the discrepancies between reality and communist propaganda, Symonenko's poems took on an ever more social context. His poems recited in front of university auditoriums were copied and widely distributed through samizdat (underground publishing, which usually meant they were typed on typewriters) and also found their way abroad to the diaspora. By the time the Soviet censors realized what was happening, it was too late. All the same, to make up for lost time, all his articles and works were stopped from being published and he suffered persecution.

He wrote his last work, *A Fairy Tale About Dupe*, only three months before his death, and it was obviously not meant for publication. The tale was overtly anti-Soviet, and it was only published in the late 1980s, in the final agonizing years of the communist regime.

With time Symonenko's poetry has not lost its appeal or its currency. For he writes about eternal things, such as love and honour, morals, patriotism, love and respect toward one's native culture and language. The sincerity of his emotions has stood the test of time, and he is no less popular today than he was in Soviet times.

Although better known for his poetry, Symonenko also wrote some short stories and a novella, which have been translated for this collection of his prose. Some of these were first published in Lviv in 1965 by Kameniar Publishers under the title *Vyno z troiand* (Wine from Roses). His prose works were very succinct and in them he often criticized negative human traits. Symonenko swept across the night sky of Ukraine like a bright meteorite and left everyone in awe. Although he himself was always skeptical about the importance of his works. His diary, though not voluminous, provides an insight into the creative talent of the man; smuggled out of Ukraine after his death, it was first published in the magazine *Suchasnist* in Munich in 1965.

In translating Symonenko, I was able to gain a better insight into the author and his work by spending time living in Cherkasy: for a short period in Soviet times and rather more extended visits in post-independence times. I marvel that in this grey provincial centre such great poetry was able to be written, which proves once again that you don't have to always be in the hub of life to create great literature. Although Symonenko was offered the chance to move to the capital Kyiv by various writer friends, he refused and chose to live and work as a journalist on a provincial newspaper, 'to be closer to the people'.

Yuri Tkacz

Rose Petal Wine

Even the ancient old men stared at her, and rarely did any young fellow walk past without eyeing her from head to foot. The gazes of some glowed with rapture, while others burned with undisguised desire, and still others admired her, as if she were a work of art. When she tossed her black plaits onto her resilient breasts and sailed through the village with a hoe over her shoulder, the boys went wild. They fearfully approached her gate and fervently told her of their love for her, but she merely listened and said nothing. No one dared touch her, as if afraid to defile her beauty. She showed them no scorn and never put any of them down, only begging them, when they were leaving:

"Please don't come to see me anymore. All right?"

And her sloe eyes brimmed with such entreaty, that no one dared contradict her. Each boy's intoxication with her beauty passed, they fell in love with ordinary snub-nosed or sharp-nosed girls, and Olha remained a pleasant memory for them.

Andriy never dared approach her. What chance did he have, a lame hunchback, when fellows far more handsome than him got the flick from her. She often caught his gaze and always beamed affably in reply; however, he took it to be offensive pity.

The boys became tractor drivers and chauffeurs, went off to join the air force or navy, while he couldn't even dream of such things. He pottered about in the collective-farm orchard and grew flowers at home.

He was attracted to flowers after his mother had passed away. There wasn't a single vegetable in his yard, only grapevines, apple trees, sour cherries, and flowers, lots of flowers. And his mother's grave was covered in flowers from early spring until Indian summer, like a raised flowerbed.

He gave lavish bunches of flowers to brides, and everyone was grateful to him, and everyone respected him for it, while he longed to taste at least one droplet of love himself.

"Will you give me a bunch of flowers for my wedding too?" Olha once asked when they were picking apples in the orchard.

He nearly went numb from surprise, but nevertheless replied:

"You can choose whichever ones you want yourself." Then he took courage and said: "I've got lots of them. And if you like, I can make some wine from rose petals for your wedding."

"Wine from roses?" she expressed amazement. "What a fib."

"You don't believe me?" he grew agitated. "The wine is like tenderness. When you come to pick your flowers, I'll give you some to taste."

And he hobbled off to his lean-to, answering to the calls of the caretaker.

For some reason Andriy genuinely believed that Olha would come for the flowers. He waited for her each evening. His anxiety was even sensed by the neighbourhood boys, who chirped each evening in his yard. These were Andriy's most loyal friends and trustworthy custodians of his flowers and orchard. Anyone who dared pick even a bunch of grapes or a flower was subjected to unmerciful ostracism. They were hounded relentlessly and cruelly, as only children were capable of doing.

Each evening these shaven-haired horticulturalists mobbed Andriy like flies. He told them how he dreamt of flowers, how they whispered to the grey stars, he dreamed up fairy tales about wondrous lands where flowers were not only fragrant, but also spoke and walked and played hide-and-seek, and wilted only when an unhappy person appeared in that land.

"Flowers love happy people. In our land they don't wilt but cry from unhappiness. Have you seen how much dew covers them in the morning? That's their tears. Anyone who finds a dry flower on a dew-drenched morning will be incredibly happy."

"And have you ever found a dry flower?"

"No, I haven't, and probably never will…"

A kind and sincere sky hung over them, and the youngsters felt that it wasn't at all covered in stars, but in flowers, and that these fairy-tale flowers had been planted by uncle Andriy.

Olha came on Sunday morning. She was so beautiful, that all the flowers seemed to hang their heads, while their master felt utterly useless and didn't know where to hide.

"Is it true that a dry flower found on a dewy morning will bring you happiness?" she asked Andriy.

The lad's tongue stuck to his palate, his eyes froze in wonder.

"Who… Where d'you hear this?"

"I came here yesterday evening and heard you telling the children. So, is it true or not?"

"No. I just made that up," Andriy buried his eyes in a paeony bush.

Olha sighed.

"It's a pity I can't dream up such lovely things."

'Why d'you need all this?' the lad wondered. 'You've got your beauty your mother endowed you with. While I… What will I do when I can no longer make up these strange stories?'

A little while later they sat in the arbour, overgrown with hops and wild grape, and tasted the rose-petal wine.

"You're a very nice lad, Andriy," Olha said.

"You meant that I'm a good person?" he asked her.

"I meant what I said," Olha laughed and began to fret for no obvious reason. "Many fellows tell me that I'm beautiful and that's why they love me. They think it makes me feel good. But is it my fault that I'm beautiful? Is my beauty – me?"

She playfully tossed her plaits from behind onto her breasts.

"I want someone to fall in love with me and not my beauty, my black eyebrows and red cheeks." She noticed that Andriy was trying to say something and began to speak even faster: "What good is beauty? The wind withers your skin, the rain washes away your rouge! You lug around heavy crates in the barn, bend your back double in the beetroot fields – and soon there's nothing left of your beauty…"

She grew silent and Andriy did not know what to say.

"Well, tell me, Andriy, when bad weather and work shrivel me up, will I still be loved by the one who falls for my beauty?"

"I don't know, Olha," the lad sighed sincerely. "I don't know of anyone who could not love you as you are!"

"I won't be like this all my life, Andriy," she said sorrowfully. "So, can I pick myself some flowers?"

Andriy nodded and the girl waded into the living lake of colour. She walked among the flowers and his enamoured eyes followed her. Olha must have carefully examined almost every single petal and returned to the arbour empty-handed.

"It was a pity to pick any of them," she admitted in embarrassment. "They're so beautiful. I'd best come another time. Is that alright?"

He saw her to the gate and said nothing. The girl walked out into the street and, looking into the blue unrest of his eyes, said softly:

"You must make some rose-petal wine before the wedding…"

13.6.1962

Roosters Crowed on the Sashes

Onyska's legs turned to wood whenever she heard his voice ring out somewhere nearby. She always walked past him barely breathing and did not dare move even an eyebrow in his direction.

And Viktor would yell:

"Onyska! When will you tell me that I am the one for you?"

"After you've milked a full bucket of milk from a billy goat," the girl shot back in reply.

"I won't go running after you," the fellow sneered. "I'll simply come to ask for your hand in marriage."

"Come around then, we've had a good harvest of pumpkins[1] this year," she uttered the words as if passing them through a sieve, holding both her outrage, her pain and her hope behind her white teeth.

Sometimes the milkmaids were fed up and began to defend Onyska.

"You're not even worthy of her little pinkie!" they told him.

"Oh, yeah! All I need say is 'chicky-chick', and she'll come running like a chicken," the accountant did not relent.

"Take care you won't have to sit on the eggs yourself afterwards," Onyska shot back to uproarious laughter.

Onyska could only confide in her father what that undue familiarity of hers cost her. Her father was still very young. He had gone off to war aged thirty and had remained like that forever. Onyska often wanted to see him grey-haired and sporting a moustache. But it never worked. Mother had befriended old age, but father remained young. Time had lost its power over him.

"Oh, how hard it is for me, dad," Onyska said, dropping the black sorrow of her plaits to her waist. "How I love him and how

---

[1] The offering of a pumpkin by a girl signified refusal, when the lad came to ask for her hand in marriage.

I... detest him!" she stamped her small foot. "What should I do, dad?"

But her father remained silent and then the arches of her girlish eyebrows slipped down to her snub nose and her eyelashes blinked ever so fast, forcing the disobedient tears back inside.

Autumn dawns are uneasy, like delirium. Onyska felt their grey bottomlessness with her sleepy eyes and dived into their unease. On the way to the farm she finished watching her girlish dreams.

Once she was woken from her daydreams by Viktor.

"Why are you stumbling off to, like some lunatic?" he burst out laughing right beside her ear and Onyska again felt her legs go numb. But neither her head nor her tongue ever went numb.

"Better tell me why you've crawled out of your diapers so early this morning?"

He said nothing and then somehow shyly took her by the hand. Onyska felt no desire to wrench her hand free.

"I never thought your hands would be so tender..."

"A peasant won't believe anything, till he's felt it," she hid her disappointment in a smile.

"Will you be mine?" Viktor suddenly blurted out of the blue. "Will you?"

"Maybe I will... go to work in a mine," she managed to free her hand from his and walked along, as if on sharp knives.

"Then I'll come round to ask for your hand in marriage," he said, as if he had not heard her words and, just as suddenly as he had appeared, he melted into the transparent grey air.

For a whole week, no matter where she went, Onyska was pursued by whispers and giggles. Under the frank curious gazes her shoulders hunched over and insult weighed heavily on her thoughts. "He's gone and blabbed to the whole village". Her chest was constricted with suffering.

Viktor came on the Saturday. His cap pushed to one side, in shining chrome leather boots, handsome and sleek like a poster boy.

15

He sat down on the bench, swung one leg over the other, as if showing off his new boots.

And he immediately began some idle chit-chat with her mother. He spoke a long time, boasting overtly, and then said, as if among other things:

"Auntie, I've come to ask for your Onyska's hand in marriage…"

Her mother looked up in surprise and said in an offended tone:

"Do people negotiate with the parents about such things these days, Viktor? Onyska has her own head on her shoulders." And, as if emphasizing her lack of concern for what was taking place in the house, she slowly tottered outside into the yard.

For a long time, the two of them sat in the house and said nothing. The roosters crowed on the sashes and their silent song filled the ears with ringing.

"So, what have you to tell me, Onyska?" Viktor's voice splashed out anxiously.

'You haven't asked me anything yet."

"You know why I'm here." He looked at her with such entreaty and such guilt that her entire body filled with a sultry craving.

"You haven't even trampled a path to my gate and already you're knocking at my heart," she tried to shake the languid feeling permeating her body.

"But you love me…"

"How do you know?" she raised her scoffing eyes.

"The whole village says so…"

"But the one person who matters hasn't said anything," Onyska threw her embroidery into a corner and didn't know what to do with her hands. Her brown eyes flashed with anger. Viktor seemed to see her for the first time.

"So, you're willing to make a fool of me in front of the whole village?" he asked and immediately realized the absurd wretchedness of his question.

"What a strange fellow you are, Viktor," tears seemed to flow from her lips. "When you leave here pick as many pumpkins from the garden as you like. You can even bring a cart to collect them," Onyska seemed to mock her own suffering. "One won't be enough for you, take a whole cartful and go feast your arrogance on them…"

He left doubled over, as if he was carrying a whole cart filled with pumpkins on his back.

And meanwhile Onyska sat sobbing over her embroidery.

17-24.3.1962

The Black Horseshoe

The clouds hung so low that passers-by emerged from them unexpectedly and just as unexpectedly dived back into them. The girl had lifted her head, as if trying to poke her gaze through their swirling sullenness. Her long eyelashes touched the edges of the clouds, while her eyes were the only blue splotches in the surrounding overcast greyness.

"I don't love you," the girl said, staring into the sky. "You lied to me…"

"No, I didn't …"

"You didn't love me."

He was staring at the ground, unaware of what was happening above them.

"I love you," the lad nervously scraped his shoe on the grassy knoll and had already left the imprint of a black horseshoe in it. "I love you…"

"You're simply afraid of losing me and being left alone."

"Rubbish!" he suddenly burst out. "If you feel indifferent toward me, then…"

She let fly two blue bolts of lightning at him.

"Why do you keep staring at the ground?"

With difficulty he raised his eyes, as if they were heavy weights, and cast a furtive glance at her, but a moment later his eyes were again buried in the grass.

"It makes no difference where I look."

"You never look me in the eye. You're always greedy and impatient," she tore his doubts to shreds. "You didn't want to be happy with me, you only wanted to make me happy."

She suddenly burst into tears and could barely stop herself from pressing against his chest.

"I too want to make at least one person happy," she said, angrily pushing her heel deep into the soft earth and impetuously made off.

"Wait!" he chased after her.

The thunder had a long fit of coughing and large drops began to slap against the leaves. Two people emerged from the clouds. They were holding hands and were making a beeline for the maple tree. Drenched and short of breath, they were happy to be under its dense canopy.

"Look, a horseshoe," the lad exclaimed.

They squatted around the black semicircle soldered into the green madness. And somehow their eyes met unexpectedly, then their hands and lips.

"Horseshoes bring luck," her lips rustled.

Those who find horseshoes never think of those who lost them.

17.3.1962

He Stopped Her from Sleeping

At times, his chest was racked by long fits of coughing. Because of his smoking.

"Hnat, I'm sick and tired of your smoking!" she would yell from the bedroom. "You're stopping me from sleeping."

He would look guiltily at the brown curtains and say:

"All right, Li, I won't cough any more."

"You can go into the kitchen and cough there till morning, if you like!" the woman he called Li drawled sweetly.

The light moved with him into the poky kitchen. Before dawn, it would become exhausted and die away. He too grew tired. His short nervous sleep was filled with phantasmagorical monsters. In the past he had made fun of positive heroes depicted in crappy novels. Workbenches or tractors always appeared as positive heroes in his dreams. He would dream of every girl, except Li. How he missed her, even in his dreams!

Now he dreamed of formulae, parallel bold lines and the chief designer's pipe. Although Yakym Ivanovych had never smoked a pipe, in his dreams Hnat always positively knew that the pipe belonged to the fellow. He mentioned this once to Yakym Ivanovych.

"All right, I'll put it in my pipe and smoke it," the fellow said, joking. "Anyway, such dreams have some basis. You must be exhausted."

Yakym Ivanovych liked Hnat, but he did not show his feelings, so that there would be no idle gossip. To his own amazement, he had asked that time:

"Do you argue often with Lida?"

"No, we never argue…"

"And she never snaps at you?"

"Sometimes. But only when I stop her from sleeping…"

"I suspected you stopped her from sleeping," Yakym Ivanovych quipped, and his kind brown eyes suddenly began to turn grey. This happened each time he was angry.

"My God, what have you done to the kitchen!" Lida would be horrified each morning when she surveyed the piles of cigarette butts. "You'll soon become skinny as a rake…"

Hnat loved his smoke-filled nights. He loved his cigarettes, his coughing fits, and his drafting implements. Of course, he could have done without the coughing, but not without those nights! He relished his exhaustion and his wild dreams. And his wife's sleepy mutterings.

"Haven't you had enough of those stinking cigarettes?"

Lida failed to understand his cigarettes, or his coughing, or his dreams. And she did not like his exhaustion or his nights up alone.

When Hnat was able to gather his thoughts, when his sleeplessness gave birth to a whimsical web of drawings, he would race into the bedroom and grab Lida by the shoulders:

"Li, how great everything has turned out…"

"What are you babbling about?" she would ask in sleepy lassitude.

"Li, I found what I was seeking!"

"But, darling, does that mean you have to rouse the whole city?"

He would sit in the kitchen till morning and kill the taste of her indifference with tobacco smoke. In the morning he would pack his things into a suitcase and throw insults at her. She would weep and reply in kind.

And then one day he appeared in the doorway of the office of his father-in-law, aka the chief designer, and let loose his outrage:

"I've left her so that she can have her beauty sleep. I'll go up North and never come back…"

Yakym Ivanovych's eyes were grey, but his voice sounded indifferent:

"Go and start work. No need to begin snivelling here," Yakym Ivanovych said. And grew silent.

21

In the evening he turned up at Hnat's desk:

"Lida came to see me…"

Hnat tossed back his black shock of hair and looked at his father-in-law as if from a deep pit:

"What did she say?"

"Only things that women usually say in such circumstances." He ran his eyes over his son-in-law's awkward figure and must have been thinking about something very distant. "I told her that when people love each other they don't take their tears to intermediaries."

Hnat began to dress and had problems slipping his left shoe into his galosh. They took the stairs from the third floor, smoking as they went.

An autumn wind was wreaking havoc outside. They walked through its uproarious laughter.

Unexpectedly Yakym Ivanovych grabbed Hnat's shoulder and swung him around to face him:

"I told her you might return once she wakes up to herself. Then you won't stop her from sleeping."

He went off, almost running away from Hnat.

Hnat came to the hotel and went to bed very early. He dreamed of Lida, parallel lines and the chief designer's non-existent pipe.

27-28.11.1962

Opanas Krokva's Wedding

Nobody understood what the lanky and scraggly German was babbling about. But everyone saw snakes crawling from his mouth. They hissed for a long time in everyone's ears, and then the hissing was translated into human language by the frightened teacher from the neighbouring village:

"He says that on the outskirts of your settlement yesterday evening three soldiers were shot dead. If this had happened here, the Germans would have executed every single one of you. As it is, they want to hang only those with partisans in the family. If you don't name the families of the partisans, you will all be killed."

Two hundred grandpas, grandmas, women, and children stood in the insanely hot sun, but they were cold. Spurts of frost squirted from the black barrels of the automatic rifles and machine-guns, aimed at everyone and no one in particular. A pre-harvest sultriness and a pre-death silence hung over the crowd. And then snakes again issued forth from the SS officer's mouth.

"He says you can remain silent for another ten minutes and then he'll give the order to fire."

For ten minutes wrinkles played on foreheads, for ten minutes the sun dripped silence, for ten minutes people stared with numb eyes at the deformed knotgrass, as if seeking salvation in it. Then the crowd began to stir, and a small aggregation of people regurgitated the thousand-year-old Opanas Krokva. He even forgot to bow before the people and made straight for the teacher.

"Tell this boar that my sons killed those bastards. And tell them also not to dare beat me, because I've got the mange. Let them simply hang me."

"How many of your sons are in the forest?" the teacher translated the SS officer's question.

"Every single one of them."

"Who is left at home?"

"There was the old lady, but she passed away."

"May your tongue wither!" a grey old woman's figure emerged from the crowd, looking perhaps a century younger than the old fellow. "Placing me alive into the grave and in public too. You won't escape me, you devil, not even into the next world!"

The SS officer guffawed long and hard, when the teacher translated the old woman's monologue to him.

"Is she your old lady?" he asked Opanas.

"Aha. Mine. Whose else."

"Is it true, what grandpa said, that your sons are in the partisans?" he quizzed the old woman.

"It's the truth. Would someone like him lie? All our falcons are roosting in the forest..."

They were hung on a giant elm next to the small former church. With amazed eyes they looked at the people they had saved and poked out their bitten blue tongues at the German avengers.

Opanas Krokva had never had any children and grandma Orysia, who had tied the knot with him through the hangman's rope, had never been his wife. People said that when they were young, they were very much in love and wanted to marry, but her parents would not let them and married Orysia off to a richer man.

Maybe this was true, or perhaps people's fantasies were creating a new legend about true love, which had manifested itself on their deathbed.

undated

A Ballad About Grandpa

I was sitting with my back against the barn while grandpa was competing with the sun in the meadow, to see who would be the first to complete their daily chores. A long shadow from the hill was already licking at his left foot, while his right one was still stepping along a ribbon of sunlight. The sharp scythe was whistling away – grandpa was impatient to finish mowing the last bit of meadow and finally rest. The shadows reached his knees, then suddenly jumped to his waist, thereupon making their way up to his chest.

I rose to my feet and stood on my tippy toes.

"Ivanko!" grandpa's voice reached me. He was now up to his neck in shadows and wiping the scythe with a handful of mown grass. "Can you hear me, Ivanko?"

"No," I yelled, cupping my hands around my mouth.

"So why are you answering me then, you lazybones?" Grandpa's voice was calm, and I knew that he wasn't at all angry with me. "Fetch my tobacco pouch, else the mosquitoes will eat me alive."

Grandpa was obviously trying to frighten me. The mosquitoes could never have gobbled him up, because grandpa was very big and a hundred times stronger than all the mosquitoes in our marsh. I really enjoyed doing things for grandpa. I dashed off across the vegetable patch to grandpa's jacket and fetched the tobacco pouch from his pocket, ran out onto the mown meadow and, jumping over the neat rows of mown grass, raced off toward him.

"Watch your feet," I heard grandpa's instructions. "You're belting along like a frightened hare."

"Are frightened hares really fast?"

"Of course, they're fast."

"So that even you couldn't catch one?"

"Don't know, never tried."

"Why not?"

Grandpa licked his cigarette and a sly smile appeared under his moustache:

"Because they don't give you workdays[2] for that."

"And if they did?"

"Wouldn't do it, all the same. I don't like doing stupid things."

The answer failed to satisfy me, and I unleashed a torrent of questions at grandpa.

"Hey, hey!" laughed his creased lips. "Better grab the scythe and take it into the barn."

We walked across the mown meadow and the sky darkened above us, the earth buzzed in a thousand different ways and I listened to grandpa's words. An invisible force poured into my heart, which would tie me down for ever and ever to this land and to this melodic peaceful language.

…The more grandpa's hair was peppered with frost, the more he loved me and the more he revealed his spiritual treasury to me. He grew old before my eyes and it seemed to him that his strength and even his very life were flowing into me, for grandpa had no sons – they had been mowed down by plagues and bullets…

"You're my snub-nosed little immortality," grandpa would whisper when I fell asleep to the music of his words.

They were nice words, for grandpa never used bad language with me.

I often insulted and offended grandpa either because of my ineptitude or cruel childish egotism. But grandpa magnanimously forgave me, as only great people can forgive. And grandpa was great both in his frankness and in that he didn't wheedle more than he deserved from life.

Grandpa loved to read history and geography books, as well as Shevchenko and Gorky, because he considered Shevchenko a peasant writer, while Gorky was an urban writer.

---

[2] Villagers on collective farms were not paid a wage, but credited days they had worked, and were then issued grain or other commodities as payment.

"No one else writes the truth like they do. Others are clever too, but not as good. They don't have the intelligence of either a peasant or a working man. If I haven't understood them, then ask them to forgive me, when you grow up."

Forgive him, then, Count Tolstoy and Anton Chekhov, don't take offence at him, mighty [Ivan] Franko and gentle Lesia [Ukrainka], don't be angry Aleksandr Blok, Vladimir Mayakovsky and Oleksandr Dovzhenko. And many more of you. And those who saw, how he tore food from his own mouth, to give every last grain for the war effort, how he fed his grandchildren on 300-gram workdays[3] – those who saw this and remained silent or chirruped rhymes about love, let them visit his grave and ask his forgiveness. They failed to fathom either his strength, or his beauty, or his work. And if he refuses to forgive them, then they should burn their books and take on other work, so that they are not poor in old age.

[Grandpa was a contemporary of many great men. He fed them with his bread and for this alone he earned the right to have a monument erected in his memory.]

...I was in grade eight back then. It was a nine-kilometre walk to school. For my fourteen years, it wasn't all that close.

On Sundays grandpa read all day long. About geography, most probably.

"Ivan, go and split some firewood," mother said.

"Why me?"

"Because I can't anymore," grandpa replied.

"All you do is read books!"

"Stop mouthing off, Ivan!" mother scolded me. "You're only good with your tongue."

I was hacking away at the green osier near the woodpile. Grandpa walked past me on his way to the barn. In his hand dangled a stiff hemp tether. I hacked at the osier, while everything was quiet in the barn.

---

[3] Villagers were often paid in grain, calculated at 300 grams for each day they worked on the collective farm.

Suddenly I felt as if someone had struck my heart with the butt-end of an axe. I tossed the axe into the snow and dashed into the barn.

"Grand-pa!"

He was standing and mixing some mash for the cow. And from the manger Lyska the cow was greedily following his every move, bound with the stiff tether. Grandpa looked at me and, seeing the fear in my face, became worried himself.

"What's wrong, Ivan?"

"You took the tether and I thought…"

I pressed against his ancient sheepskin coat, howling like a small child, and asked his forgiveness.

In the evening grandpa said:

"Hanna, let Ivanko stay home from school tomorrow."

"Why?"

"If I'm asking you, then there's a reason."

"All right, Ivanko can stay home," mother shrugged her shoulders.

But it was no whim. On Monday grandpa was no longer with us. Stern and beautiful, he lay in a coffin on our ancient oak bench. And outside the sun was shining, the snow squeaked underfoot, and the roosters were crowing in advance of an approaching thaw.

…I love old men more than anyone else. They are the living wisdom, the unwritten history of our nation. On their hunched shoulders they bear so much beauty and tenderness, that everyone envies them.

And when I see some grey-haired old fellow on the bus with a bundle of bagels, I immediately imagine him coming home, getting out his simple gift and saying to his small grandson, Ivanko:

"Look what I brought you from the bunny…"

He sits his black or blond-haired little immortality on his knees, and the fellow listens open-mouthed to his ingenious grandpa's account, which will be a wickerwork of reality and fantasy. And

28

one day his grandfather's beauty will inevitably awaken in him too, and he will feed on his grandfather's wisdom and language.

9.3.1962

The Incredible Interview

That morning Shvoren was woken by the telephone. Opanas grabbed the receiver.

"Yes."

"Shvoren? I'm calling from *Poetical Miscellany*. Our correspondent will come to visit you shortly. Meet him in full kit."

Opanas threw down the receiver and loaded his popgun.

Soon an awkward and greasy youth burst into the room. His ruddy face was scratched and covered in pimples. He looked timid, but insolent.

"Good morning! Time to face the music. Didn't expect me? So here I am – crawled in through the window with my delicate body and standing at attention before you."

"Who are you?" Opanas yelled out wildly, bewildered by the appearance of this total degenerate.

"I'm a reporter. A hybrid of poetry and prose, the newspaper's illegitimate son. Clear? I think in images. Everything I have said to date can be found in my book *Lacquered Dirt*. Try to understand."

"Aren't you from *Poetical Miscellany*?" Shvoren finally chose a pause in the tirade.

"I besprinkle the poetical palette there. My first question is: where, when and how were you born?"

Shvoren opened his mouth, but the bastard wouldn't relent:

"My mother didn't give birth to me, I was born of my own accord. My talent is made of machine muscles, my head is a laboratory labyrinth. I am cutting-edge science. I stand by the roadside in yellow milkweed – I've done time in the clinker. *Da*, it happened. Eh, a giraffe glides over the rye fields. By the way, where did you spend your childhood?"

"I was bo…"

"Aha. I clean forgot. Beside the house I stand feeding hungry geese with an empty heart. They say it's a pun. Allow me to ask you, what is talent? Don't know? Well, there. Talent is…. Wait, I've gone off on a tangent. Right, so where did you study?"

The talkative bastard had no intention of shutting up.

"I know my time will come and it will rest its heavy hands upon my fluttering shirt. What? I'm amazed at your indiscretion. How dare you interrupt a guest, especially one like me. Aha! I've recognized you by your voice and sound! I step across fish-laden country and remove my boots to dry. Good, eh? I envy myself. Do you know this one: the hay reeks of cosmos and bronze, from which a smithy is forging a monument to me? No, you wouldn't get it."

Shvoren's hands had begun to shake and he was working out a plan of action.

"What are you working on now?" the 'terrorist' kept up his tirade. "I hear with my eyes, my ears see all, the universe rests on the palm of my hand."

He came up to the mirror on the wall, peered into it and asked in surprise:

"Is this some thief? Or murderer? Or robber?"

"He's a genius," Shvoren hissed.

"Really? And I thought only I…"

"Give him your hand," Shvoren suggested. The 'terrorist' turned toward the mirror and offered his hand. Shvoren struck him over the head with a glass carafe and pushed him out the door.

For a minute or so there was silence. Then the door began to creak under strong blows and a life-affirming poem broke through the newly made cracks:

> Stars crowed in the corn,
> Sirius perched upon the stile,
> In a blanket of sky tattooed with stars
> I took Kyiv home to show my love.

Shvoren had no choice. He stopped writing poems. And his double never appeared again.

undated

31

Smiles Never Offend Anyone

All day long the trees swept the skies with their green brooms and finally toward evening the sun appeared from behind the clouds. It was large and mortified. The storm had washed away the weariness not only from beauteous nature – I too could almost physically feel joy budding inside my chest. A kind of unexplained and utterly giddy joy.

I sat on the bench in the small square and smiled at the trees, the sun, the bedraggled clouds, and the passers-by. Then a girl sat down beside me. Overcome with joy, she too greedily took in with her eyes the beauty of the approaching evening. Invisible patches of dampness had wearily rested upon her impenetrably dark eyebrows, which gave them an ever so slight tinge of grey and made them exquisitely beautiful.

"Why are you smiling?"

She looked at me in amazement and replied:

"How do I know?"

We sat there and smiled at everyone and everything, and I smiled at her a little bit, and she smiled back at me a tiny bit. And we felt wonderful and overjoyed, and there was nothing between us except for wordless sincerity.

And then a grey-haired fellow sat down on our bench and began to offer his evening smile to all and sundry. He wasn't in our way and we weren't in his – there was enough room for all our smiles.

"My god, how shameless young people have become now!" a passer-by stopped beside us, brimming with anger. It created such a dissonance amid the evening joy, that it even upset my non-musical ears. But I smiled at him and replied:

"You're not referring to us, I hope…"

"Of course, I'm referring to you!" the passer-by stamped his foot.

"I'm sorry, but we're not doing anything."

"How can you show your happiness to the whole world so brazenly?"

"We aren't happy," the girl smiled at him. "We're only filled with joy."

"And each of us has his own joy, what's more," I added.

"You are insulting people, you cast a shadow on today's youth by your behaviour," the passer-by scolded us.

"Can a smile really offend someone or cast a shadow on someone?" I asked, not expecting a reply.

I knew that he would preach to us until he had spoilt our good mood and the evening in general. And then he would march off, so pleased with himself, as if he had indeed done something very useful.

"Why are you sitting in plain view of everyone and grinning?" he kept carrying on. "Aren't there enough secluded places where you can go?"

"Why do people have to find smiles only in secluded places?"

"Because you need to behave decently in public."

"You must think we're in love?" the girl suddenly asked.

"In any case there's some kind of hanky-panky going on between the two of you, and you needn't annoy decent people."

"But we don't even know one another!" the girl burst out laughing.

He was so taken aback that he almost turned into a stone monument.

"What? You don't even know one another? And you're sitting side by side and smiling at one another for the whole city to see?"

I thought he was going to burst with anger. He began to heap such banalities on us, that even the sun tripped up and became entangled in the tip of a poplar tree. I was ready to block my ears and to dash off, but at this moment the grey-haired fellow piped up:

"Why the hell can't you leave these young people in peace? Let them sit here and smile, they'll only offend the odd hippopotamus."

"Because of people like you who condone such action our younger generation is debauched," the defender of chastity vented his spleen at the grey-haired fellow.

"Why don't you just run along, or I'll call a militiaman," the fellow said wearily. "Boor."

"You're the one that needs to be dragged off to the militia station! Shameless lot!" the offended fellow bawled out but decided to move along all the same and a moment later his figure, bursting with indignation and prescribed truths, disappeared behind a hedge of bushes.

And we were again sitting and smiling. And the sky was guffawing so loudly, that we could see its red gums.

5.6.1962

The Grey Package

When the locomotive yanked at the carriages and Slava hopped onto the footrest, we gathered in a tight pack and began to chant at the tops of our voices:

"Hail Slava! Hail Slava!"

Slava waved us goodbye with some leaflet, yelled something to us, but we could no longer hear him and did not want to hear him – then he poked his tongue out and pulled such a face, that any monkey would have envied him.

That was how he left my life and, if he were to return, then I am sure he would be unchanged. A grey package lay in my handbag. Slava handed me this treasure on the platform and told me:

"Read it only after the train has gone quite some distance…"

This Slava was an odd, amiable sort. Because of him I endured so much misery and embarrassment, that I should have grown to hate him with every fibre in my body, as they say. Above all he disliked my mother, and she repaid him in kind so generously, that even in his presence she would say to me:

"When will you finally send this scarecrow packing?"

Slava would roar with laughter and provoke her:

"By offending me you offend the future, Auntie Zinet. We take over from you. When you are playing chess with Muhammad or Esau, I'll still be roaming Earth, making a solid contribution to the development of civilization…"

"My God, and this savage babbles on about civilization!" my mother exclaimed dramatically.

Slava's photo stands on my desk. I had asked him to give it to me. Mother hates it, because Slava looks almost alive on it. With a sly twinkle he stares sullenly at our dwelling and it seems that his large lips are about to break into a smile. I made the small wart near his nose into a cute brown mole and this made Slava look even more odd.

…We all came back to my apartment from the railway station and then for a long time the Radiola crackled away and glasses tinkled, but nothing was the same as before. Maybe it was the case only for me – while everyone else felt that things hadn't changed. Perhaps everyone else had said their goodbyes to Slava forever back at the railway station. Perhaps he hadn't offended the others the way he had offended me with that monkey face he pulled. I expected him to at least say goodbye nicely to me. The bastard!

After everyone had finally left, I plonked onto the sofa, exhausted, and ripped open the package. I ripped it open and pulled out an envelope! An ordinary plain envelope with a four-copeck stamp. I wanted to kill the teacher who had taught Slava to write so beautifully and so ca-lli-gra-phi-ca-lly. The words on the envelope said: 'Open only if you love me.' Slava wrote this warning in terrible handwriting. His hand had not shuddered a single time. Some philologist!

First, I threw the envelope onto the floor and angrily trampled it with my feet. I paid the bastard back for the four long years that he had taken out of my life. Taken them so arbitrarily, so treacherously and hell knows why. Four empty, worthless years! For one thousand four hundred and sixty-one days he had annoyed me only to finally present me with this pathetic envelope worth all of five kopecks!

But then I grabbed the envelope and ripped it open. Not to throw it away, but simply to pull out the microscopic sheet of paper inside. It read:

'For another year you will be collecting the autographs of examiners in your score book. I will wait for you for one year (The cheek! I waited four years for you! One thousand four hundred and sixty-one days), although I don't know if you will have the courage to leave Kyiv because of some hare-brained charlatan. But I'll wait anyway. I love you insanely! Slava.'

And that was that. Not a word more. I couldn't even find a single smudge on this cold piece of paper. He really was insane. I would buy him a straitjacket tomorrow and send it by express post. Let him wear it, the bugger!

Could he already have bedded down on his third-class hard bench in the train and fallen asleep…?

27.02.1963

The Psychological Joust

The literary crowd always gathered at Opanas Shvoren's place. The unacknowledged geniuses sat down at a round table and began their discussions. These verbal jousts were so heated, that in half an hour or so the room filled with smoke. And there was no smoke without fire.

One time when the assembled writers had opened their mouths to astound the world with their great new thoughts, Shvoren jumped up from his chair (actually, he had borrowed it from his neighbour) and rattled off:

"Friends! I propose we start a competition."

"How?" the humorist raised his head.

"Hm," an adherent of Remarque struck a match.

"What?" the poet commented indifferently, ready at any moment to flaunt his talents.

"Go on," concluded the realist.

"Listen then." Shvoren had wanted to get up on his chair, but his neighbour, who was standing in the doorway, waved an electric iron at him and Opanas was forced to continue with his feet planted firmly on the floor. "Yesterday I overheard two love-birds saying their goodbyes. What do you think the girl said to the boy? I bet you can't guess. She asked him, practically begged him, not to catch the bus, but to accompany her on foot. So then, each of you must logically substantiate the reason for her request. And the person closest to the truth – wins."

"Who's going to be the judge?" the realist could not restrain himself from asking.

"I'll bring the girl in question here," Shvoren explained. "Who's first?"

Everyone grew silent. A minute later the poet stood up and rolled his eyes. He belonged to the modernist school which, to spite those who wrote without using any punctuation marks, created beauty by employing only such symbols.

"Dash, bracket, exclamation mark,
An attractive question mark,
Three hyphens, four commas –
And the truth is evident."

"A work of genius!" exclaimed Shvoren and began to clap so energetically that he gave a hell of a fright to the ginger cat sleeping in the middle of the table, being the only thing decorating its surface.

After this Remarque's adherent took the floor:

"She knew that he had drunk a lot of wine and beer that evening. So that he would need to get off the bus at every stop. Especially since he had a weak bladder."

The satirist didn't leave everyone waiting long:

"He had no residency registration and, besides, he was drunk. The girl was worried that if he caught the bus he might be detained by the militia. She must have been dealing in some kind of black-market goods."

Having scratched his head a little longer than was necessary, the realist blurted out in a single breath:

"She was jealous of the attentions he might receive from the female conductor on the bus."

No sooner had he raised his hand to his head again, than the humorist fired away:

"The two of them worked together. She was very stingy. And she was afraid the lad might fall under the bus. In that case each of his co-workers would have had to donate a *karbovanets* toward a wreath for his funeral, and she had no desire to part with such money."

The phenomenal witticism made Shvoren laugh so much that he began to hiccup. Finally, pulling himself together and reigning in his hearty laughter, Opanas addressed his female neighbour:

"Tell us now, Pasha, which of them was the closest to very-tee?"

"I don't understand what berry tea has to do with this," Pasha replied. "Why the stupid question?"

"I'm asking you, who out of all of them was the closest to the truth?"

"They all spoke such utter nonsense! I asked the boy not to get on the bus so that he might stay with me till dawn. And the last bus left really early – at one a.m. Get it?" Pasha replied and, poking her tongue out at the assembled geniuses, dashed outside.

Undated

White Apparitions

White apparitions entered the lobby, stamping their awkward feet, clapping their hands, and milk-coloured flakes settled to the floor.

"What a winter!" some exclaimed, lacking the imagination to utter anything more original.

"Greetings from Grandpa Frost!" others tried joking, as they tossed their moist coats across the cloakroom counter.

Lina smiled at them superficially, for she had to be courteous. 'They're all so boring and uninteresting,' the thought kept spinning about inside her head. The boring types and the nonentities ascended the stairs to the dance hall and set about monotonously polishing the parquetry floor, flirting with equally boring and dull girls. Or else they coalesced into groups and chattered away light-heartedly about goodness knows what.

No, Lina felt no disdain toward them. She merely felt sorry for these haughty turkeys who, day in and day out, squandered their time and energy on these fandangos. Yes, fandangos, for she dared not call that shuffling of theirs dancing.

"What are you thinking about, milady?" an exceptionally wheedling voice upset Lina's composure. Aha, this was the same fellow who had tried yesterday and the day before to enthral her with his witticisms and impersonations of characters from Indian films.

"Forgotten your cigarettes again?" she asked, evading his sugary sweet smile.

"You hit the nail on the head, m'am."

"Number?" And armed with this information, Lina extracted a tattered packet of *Kazbek* cigarettes from his imported coat. There was no doubt that this gallant gentleman smoked ordinary roll-your-owns, which he made himself each night using cheap tobacco.

But how pompously he tapped his cigarette holder against the packet! How majestically he struck his match!

"Perhaps you'd like to come up with me for a dance?"

"No, I wouldn't stoop that low."

"Oh, the angel is baring her claws! Come on, how about it?"

"Listen," she said irritably, "this is a cloakroom, not some collection point for compliments gleaned from last year's films."

"Citizens, let us be mutually polite," the courteous ladies' man flung the slogan into her face.

"Visitors, please do not hinder the workers in the execution of their official duties," Lina retorted with an ultra-polite smile.

"Perhaps the lady will reveal her name to me?"

"Macbeth."

"I'll be waiting for you at the exit, then."

"If twinkle-toes has any free time, he should squander it in the company of one of the ballerinas," Lina ventured, pointing her finger upwards.

"You don't love me, you don't feel sorry for me..."

"The Society for Expressive Reading meets on Tuesdays and Fridays at three in the afternoon," she said, offering him some free information. Thank the Lord, they had begun to play the foxtrot and a string of people appeared to collect their coats.

Lina abhorred her 'profession', but she dreadfully liked to dress and undress people. There was something magical and yet incomprehensible about this, and when she finally found herself a proper job, these bouquets of human faces would continue to appear before her, eyes laughing, grieving, begging. Apart from the professional scrapers, quite a few nice boys and girls ended up here for want of something better to do. The places boredom could drive a person! Perhaps one day she too would be forced to waste away her evenings in such dance halls, dying from her partner's empty, boring conversations, hanging out for those dished-out compliments of his and dancing 'being led by him'...

At last…! The final coat had been handed out, the final 'good evening' said. She could leave for home now, but there was still so much work to do here at Auntie Pasha's. The people had trudged in snow and mud, carelessly dropped butts around the urns. Lina flitted about the foyer, while Auntie Pasha grumbled and tried to bundle her off home.

"Perhaps someone's waiting for you..."

"Then they can wait," Lina answered, rattling the dustpan, running to and fro with the broom and machine-gunning Auntie Pasha with bursts of her impressions of the evening, while the latter reproached her for being so unreasonable.

"One day you'll be itching for someone to court you, but there won't be any takers... Your girlhood years will have flowed away, like the waters of spring..."

Lina dressed hastily, at the same time convincing Auntie Pasha that she would never in her life even think of marrying, since all you ever heard these days was talk of divorces and there were so few decent young men left out there.

"Ah, go home, you sharp-nosed bundle of trouble…! You know about as much about young men, as a goat does about bulrushes..."

A white apparition was indeed waiting for her outside. He walked at her side without a trace of his previous gallantry. He mumbled something about the weather and joked clumsily. Lina's exasperation meanwhile dozed in the most secluded corners of her heart.

"I like the fact that you don't grimace and put on airs," continued the white apparition.

"Then why are you playing the dandy yourself?"

"Because..."

"Did you wait for me *because* too?"

"A wee bit *because*, and a wee bit not."

"I don't need your wee bits!"

"I do."

"Listen, are you a scoundrel, or what?" she asked, putting the question to him point-blank.

"Perhaps I am, but not too much," the fellow sighed. They became silent, walking side-by-side, each with their own thoughts.

"Perhaps I'm a fool," the not-too-much-of-a-scoundrel uttered suddenly.

"That's very likely," Lina agreed.

"Are you intelligent?"

"Who knows? Mum says I'm a shrew."

"Your mum's a great person!"

And they continued walking. The city was asleep, and the snow kept falling in thick flakes. The streetlamps looked quaint and fairytale-like because of the snow. It seemed to Lina that she was on another planet. How many riddles and surprises were awaiting her in this strange, unfamiliar, white hometown of hers?!

He didn't even dare try take her by the hand and said goodbye near the entrance to her building without begging her, like the others, to stand around with him 'for just a minute longer'.

Lina collapsed into her snow-white sheets, sighing anxiously and easily. In her dreams violet flowers grew out of her eyes.

undated

A Banquet in the Threshing Yard

Omelko Huzhko, a scrawny chatterbox, complained to the loaders in the threshing yard:

"What are they thinking in them there institutes? May the devil turn their insides out! Teaching girls all kinds of things and then they must be reckoned with. You can't say a thing, can't even swear."

The curly-haired village council secretary, Trokhym Kanivets, who had been torn away from his papers because of the harvest, noted instructively:

"Let's just say that you can live without swearing mother oaths. After all, women don't swear…"

"But that's women," Omelko twisted his chapped lips. "In our male company it's hard without that. You come to the tractor yard in the morning, and people come running from everywhere: give them this, give them that, find something for them. And where do I get all this? You can't blow it out of your nose… So, you send them all to the devil, and it makes you feel better. And the lads repay you in kind – and they cheer themselves up." He sucked on a cigarette and let out a thick cloud of smoke. "It's impossible to do without it in our line of work."

The young fellows giggled in unison. Danylo even did a little squat dance. Omelko avoided that mischievous phrase 'no way', like Muslims avoided bacon. And if it ever escaped his lips, everyone knew that the leader of the tractor brigade was in a spin about something. For No-Way was his nickname and Omelko had offered some people more than one bottle of moonshine to stop teasing him that. And many of those keen to fill up their tanks with petrol for nix played on this.

"Why are you bloody cackling there?" Omelko swore. "All the same you can't suck on any moonshine now. And what provoked my outburst, you may ask? The agronomist comes to me today and says: 'Are you even thinking when you send a tractor off to plough the fields?' 'What d'you mean?' I asked her. 'Well, because over there your Fedio is screaming from the middle of the field for someone to come save him. His tractor has stopped.' 'Eh, lady,' I explain to her, 'what we need here are not opinions, but spare parts.' 'My, my,' she plays the angel, 'I thought apart from spare parts, a clear head wouldn't go astray either.' Well, I lost it. 'There are too many of you wise guys hanging about here,' I said to the agronomist, 'but I wouldn't pay a single brand-new penny for all their brains.' Well, and then my tongue broke off its leash and I like let slip a few of my usual choice words. At first, she went red as a beetroot, but then she recovered and said: 'Even a crow can be taught to swear. But it can't fill a tractor with petrol. But you boys need to know how that's done. So, go and take Fedko some petrol. Some mechanic you are!' I nearly fell through the earth out of shame and she scoffs at me and says: 'If you swear again, I'll go and complain that you're spreading rubbish on the fields. Weeds grow because of your swearing.'"

"She's going a little too far there!" exclaimed Trokhym.

"I said as much to her," Omelko continued. "But she babbled on that it says as much in some textbook."

"Who knows, maybe she's right!" piped up the giant Danylo, who was sparing with his words. "Me dad told me that the earth likes everything clean – grain, and words, and people's consciences."

"Maybe you need to wash your hands with a bar of sand soap before working the soil?" Trokhym burst out.

"What for?" Danylo asked in utter surprise. "Are hands really dirty when soil's become ingrained in them?"

"Hands must be washed before eating. That's hygienic," Trokhym included a scientific word.

She's a straight-talking lively lass," Omelko grew enthused. "If I could dump fifteen years or so off my shoulders, I'd pass on the wife to my neighbour and make moves on the agronomist lady. But it's too late for me," the fellow sighed and once more a wave of uproarious laughter descended upon him. The whole village knew that the brigade leader was madly and furiously in love with his Olena. Once he had dared to hit her, and she grabbed their red-haired twins and dashed off to her mum's. He begged her to return, even got down on his knees, but all was in vain. Then Omelko lay down in front of the gate and said he wouldn't get up and wouldn't eat anything until Olena forgave him.

"And if you don't forgive me, I'll die. Only before I die, I'll hack off my offending fist."

He lay like a log in front of the gate for two days and two nights – just as well it was summer back then – and on the third day it began to rain. Olena took pity on him and took him back into the house.

"Oh, I'll tell auntie," Trokhym was choking with laughter, "we'll have to chop your tongue off."

"Well, she's not as stupid as you, and can tell a joke from the real thing," the brigade leader knitted his brows. "If I were in your boots, I wouldn't gape too long. You'll never come across such an amazing woman, even if you trudge all over the place for three days."

"What are you up to here uncle, matchmaking on my behalf?" the girl's throaty voice startled the men's subdued conversation. "People might think I hired you." She stood in front of the lads, flashing her hazel eyes. A smile played on her lips, while her nose was pointed provocatively up into the sky.

"I wasn't talking about you," Omelko snapped back. "How can you be beautiful, if your hair's cut short?"

Her capriciousness disappeared in a flash and another problem began to play on her pink face:

"Will there be another vehicle going to the village today?"

"We're waiting for one. There's probably enough left for one more trip," Danylo said.

Everyone felt embarrassed and remained silent. The sun dangled its red plait from beyond the horizon and the girl savoured its parting farewell. She squatted wearily on the hand thresher and looked sorrowful in the crossfire of the lads' gazes.

"In which textbook does it say that weeds grow because of swearing?" Danylo broke the silence. The girl looked at Omelko and raised an eyebrow. 'You old liar, and you said you weren't talking about me,' her gaze seemed to say triumphantly.

"I forget what the book was called. I read it ages ago." Once more she was happy and lively, and no one would have believed that the girl could ever be sad. "Why are you lads so downcast. Haven't you had lunch yet? I've got a bag full of all kinds of goodies here." She flitted down off her perch, spread out a newspaper lightning-fast and invited them: "Help yourselves, all those who aren't afraid that I'll cast a spell on them. But you must call me Tamara then, not 'the agronomist lady'. Right?"

They broke off small pieces from the chunk of bread, tossed them into their mouths and thanked her with their eyes not so much for the food, but more for her warmth.

Just as the first stars were sprouting in the sky, the first shoots of trust began to poke through the skin of wariness in their souls. The wretched crickets had already noticed this and were gossiping about it across the whole field, but the grasshoppers wouldn't believe them and sleepily jumped out onto the threshing yard to see for themselves.

By the time the long-anticipated truck had finally found the turbid threshing yard with the long eyelashes of its headlights the banquet was over, and Omelko Huzhko was handing out something very light and pleasant, because everyone was pressing forward sporting smiles as passports of their sincerity.

27.06.1962

A Naïve Young Girl

The wind gently nudged her in the back. She swung her handbag about and flirted with the wind – offering it her red cheeks or suddenly twirling about on one foot, so that it playfully outlined her demure figure. The girl sensed the curious looks of the passers-by and she obviously enjoyed this. Perhaps yesterday, or even only this morning, she had discovered the woman within her and was experiencing her discovery with trepidation.

She seemed to be born into the world a second time. Her large greyish eyes suddenly sparkled with a glistening damp sanguinity, the hempen strands of her hair seemed to grow softer and hugged her forehead, and her body became so light and obedient, that she herself was amazed that the wind was unable to lift her up on its light capacious wings and carry her off somewhere far-far away.

The girl was at that age when one is attracted to all things mysterious, unfathomable, and secretive. She was not yet aware that it was a natural instinct of youth to fall in love and to be loved. She only sensed that she craved someone very handsome and still unknown, someone without whom life was not worth living.

The girl was on her way to work. All evening long and in the morning her mother had pumped her full of instructions and fed her advice, while she only felt the incomprehensible nervous excitement inside her. So, what if it was her first time walking to work? Once before she had walked to school for the first time too, and later she had repeated this so many times that she grew bored doing it.

"Dad barely managed to find you this place," her mother lectured her. "Watch out, you hold onto it. It's clean work and the people there are nice."

Who cared that the people there were nice! As if there were no nice people elsewhere. She was standing inside the bus and everyone was watching her with such kind eyes. Could bad people have kind eyes? And would a bad person look at a good person?

She flitted out of the bus and, flirting with the white snowstorm, ran off to the plant administration building.

"Where's the plant committee head?" she asked the janitor.

"Third floor on the right, love," he said to her in a stern voice, as janitors are wont to address adults.

"I've come to start work here. My name is Oksana Oryshechko," she reported in complete seriousness to an elderly fellow with dark eyes and a bare patch in his black shock of hair.

"Aha. Very nice to meet you," the fellow retorted and measured her with his languid gaze. "I'm the head of the plant committee, Krekoten's the name – Mykola Panasovych to you."

He lit up a cigarette and asked out of the blue:

"So, where did you learn to type?"

"Mum taught me. She's a typist."

"Sit down at the typewriter."

He dictated some forty metres of thoughtless text to her from some protocol or newspaper and then cheered her up in a lacklustre voice:

"Good girl. Occasionally this will come in handy. And now file the newspapers because they're a real mess here." And he made off for his office.

Oksana hummed a song about the snow and the wind, the newspapers flapped their grey wings in her dexterous hands and obediently fell into place. With a deft twist she walked around the desk with the bound newspapers and entered his office.

"Mykola Panasovych, the newspapers have all been filed."

"Good."

For a moment or so only his heavy breathing could be heard.

"If there are any visitors, tell them I can see them from two o'clock onwards. I'm busy right now." On the desk before him lay an open magazine, his voice oozed laziness and lassitude.

"So, what do I do?" she blurted out.

51

"Don't put the cart before the horse!" he said unexpectedly. "I'll let you know when I need you."

For want of something better to do she flipped through the bound newspapers, typed a letter to her girlfriend in the village, peered with a long face into her small mirror. Occasionally she was summoned by Mykola Panasovych:

"Type up a list of the correspondence course students."

"Make a copy of this letter. In duplicate."

The day passed. The week dragged on. Monotony and boredom were wound onto the invisible reel of time. Papers rustled, her heart pumped away.

"When will I start doing something?" she asked one day.

"You're managing your duties perfectly."

"Won't I have a real job in the end?"

"A real job?" Mykola Panasovych even managed a smile. "You're a naïve little girl. Each task you do is real. That's what we are taught."

Passionately she tried to prove something to him, but he only nodded his head indulgently and reproachfully. He found her arguments ridiculous. He was a son of his time. Somehow, he had once risen up the ladder, being sucked up, and was dropped into this chair. And he remained sitting here. And he would remain sitting here without any complaints, until he was moved into another chair. As was always the case with people of low culture and wretched souls, he was never bothered by conscience. He even looked patronizingly at people, especially the restless ones, and considered himself irreplaceable. Emptiness was indeed difficult to replace with something.

"Know what, Mykola Panasovych," Oksana said to her own amazement, "I won't be turning up to work tomorrow…"

She did not listen to what he was mumbling behind her back. She was already hurrying down the stairs, her handbag tracing circles in the air, and in her bosom something immeasurably dear and gentle was awakening, wrestled from indifference.

Once more Oksana wanted people to look at her. And she indeed caught someone's eye in the bus. Aha, that black-haired fellow. He rose from his seat and offered it to her:

"Have a seat, please."

"I'm about to get off," the girl made her way to the exit, feeling his unusual gaze upon her. Before getting off, she turned around, suddenly showed the lad the tip of her tongue and hopped out onto the asphalt.

The wind picked up Oksana on its white wings, she flirted with it and did not worry at all that her mother would be fretting because of her unreasonable action.

12.6.1962

Odium

He arrived agitated and unceremonious. Without greeting anyone, he hung his grey jacket on the chair and set about wiping the sweat from his forehead with the palm of his hand.

"How long have you been working with Serhiy?"

"Two years," I replied.

He drubbed his fingers on the desk for a long time.

"I've known him since childhood. He was a good friend, but now he's become an enemy. I don't know if he'll ever forgive me."

"People often become enemies for no reason at all," I said, just so as not to remain silent.

"He has every right to detest me." I could see how difficult Borys found it to admit this. He removed several yellowed sheets of paper from his pocket, which looked like they had been steeped in nicotine, and lay them on the table.

"Is this the story of your quarrel?" I inquired.

"No, it's the wailing of his soul and, if you like, the story of my villainy."

I was taken aback by this overt self-castigation, for how could a real villain be capable of sincere repentance? Despicable people are always so sure of their might and self-righteousness.

"I don't believe in theatrical gestures," I said and saw the shadows playing across Borys' forehead. "And besides, how can I help you? I'm not about to reconcile the two of you, because Serhiy has no need of such friends."

"Serhiy has no friends, I know that for a fact. He doesn't trust anyone. No, no, don't object," he looked unblinkingly straight into my eyes. "I killed his faith in people, and you can help me restore it!" Noticing my look of annoyance and protest, he jumped up from his chair and almost burst into tears. "Don't answer, just read this first."

Cursing myself for my weakness of character, I opened the yellowed manuscript and slowly began to read the text.

I

Someone lightly touched my shoulder, then pulled away one corner of the blanket.

"He's asleep."

"Then wake him."

The voices were familiar, but my morning faintness and sleepiness stopped me from recognizing them. I hadn't the slightest intention of trying to work out who it was. But after a while my blanket slipped onto the floor and straight after this someone began to laugh loudly. Then the laughter grew quiet and a painfully familiar voice boomed near my ear:

"Serge with the urge, forever the splurge…"

I sat up in bed.

"Borys? You devil! What brings you here?"

"Aha, recognized me after all. But before you start your embraces, you'd better go and wash that mug of yours."

"And I will," I yawned and smiled, fruitlessly searching about for my slippers with my feet. "All the same, how did you make it here? I sometimes get lost in this labyrinth myself."

"I'm not surprised. With your sense of direction… Hurry up there, I've got only two days in Kyiv. You're going to have to be my tour guide."

"Oh my, how nauseating!"

My fellow classmate Viktor, with whom I rented the room, looked on perplexed and his eyes wouldn't stop blinking.

Three years earlier Borys and I had finished school and I knew him quite well enough not to deny him his whims. Kyiv interested him no more than Ancient Rome. But he mustered enough fervour to reach St Sophia Cathedral. He had a devilish sense of perception, and after we had spent ten minutes wandering about the grounds he announced boldly:

"I guarantee the domes are gold plated. And this, of course is Bohdan[4]."

Like every provincial, in order to round out the harmony of his senses, Borys enriched his impressions of the city with a hearty serving of cheap ice-cream, wolfing it down with fantastic speed and, after licking his lips, declared:

"You know, there aren't too many beautiful girls in Kyiv. There's more even in our small Lubny. Let's head for the beach."

And so, here we were at the beach. Along the way my savvy companion managed to notice that the Dnipro River was wider than the Sula, indicating that such a large mass of water made him feel suspicious and therefore he categorically refused to go swimming.

"I'll watch over your clothes and wink at the girls instead. That I know how to do. And if the truth be known, I have no underpants." This was a little bit too much information. For some reason, I wasn't overjoyed by his company, but our old friendship stopped me from unceremoniously sending him on his way.

I swam on my own and took no notice of what was happening around me. My enjoyment was interrupted by a worried voice:

"Don't swim in that direction, there's a whirlpool there! I know…"

A girl was cautioning me. I turned around and our eyes met.

"There's a whirlpool there," she repeated.

I smiled gratefully, dived underwater and surfaced right in front of her (I can see underwater, so I had no problems performing this feat).

"Thank you."

"Whatever for? You probably don't go swimming too often round here?"

"On the contrary. It's just that I'm not afraid of this whirlpool."

---

[4] Bohdan Khmelnytsky, Ukrainian Cossack leader, whose statue stands in a square outside the cathedral.

We swam side-by-side and I could hear that her breathing was nice and even.

"You're not a bad swimmer," I voiced my bold conclusion.

"You're not too bad yourself... Know what, let's see instead who can stay underwater the longest."

"Agreed. Only I don't trust girls. Especially blondes. Let's hold hands — the first to yank the other's hand is the loser."

We repeated this prank three times, and each time I won.

"You have no pity for my self-esteem," she replied, offended.

"I have my own to worry about."

The current took us downstream and we slowly approached a wide stretch of water.

"Will I see you again?" I tried to revive the conversation.

"Of course."

"Where?"

"On the silver screen. I'm an actress."

"An actress? Goodbye, then," and I turned away. She burst out laughing and quickly caught up to me.

"Are you angry at me? Why?"

"Not really. It's just that there's no point to us being acquainted."

"Don't be funny. Why's that?"

"I'm just an ordinary student. What can we have in common? You could perhaps string me along for a bit."

"And so, what if that were the case? You have nothing to lose."

"Nor anything to gain. In any case, I'm no plaything."

We stepped out onto the riverbank. This surprisingly beautiful girl annoyed me for some inexplicable reason. She was so slender and tiny, and there was something enigmatically tender about her.

"Are you an actress or a mermaid?" I asked, pointedly trying to provoke her. With feigned indifference I began to jump about on one leg to dislodge the water from my ear.

"One and the other," she said, calmly watching my anarchic antics. "Maybe you finally want to know my name?"

"Maybe, but not now. I'll wait till you become a famous film star."

"Then I'll tell you myself! And right now."

"There's no need. I'll block my ears anyway."

"You're impossible. But I won't relent until I find out, who you are."

"If you manage that, I'll be able to gauge your abilities as a sleuth."

"You're far too polite," the poor Mermaid was almost shedding tears. Obviously, nothing gets to women more than indifference.

I was overcome with unexpected joy, but I still managed to find the strength within to reply a phlegmatic 'thank-you' and headed for the riverside beach. The Mermaid walked alongside me, strumming her finger against her lips and glancing at me occasionally. Honest to God, her eyes showed more than just a sense of having been insulted.

"Serge with the urge, where you been, demiurge?" called out the temperamental custodian of my things from afar. "I'm about to die of boredom here."

"The water's really nice today," I growled dryly with dissatisfaction, settling down on the sand. The Mermaid courageously parked herself beside me.

"Who's this?" Borys was unable to contain his curiosity.

"I don't know. Probably some water nymph. I caught her in the Dnipro River."

The Mermaid maintained a haughty silence and ran her fingers through the sand.

"You could at least introduce us."

"I don't know who she is."

I turned over onto my back, covered my eyes with the palm of my hand and pretended, that I didn't give a damn whether she was there or not. After a while they began to whisper among themselves. I heard snatches of words from the conversation between my strange companion and the peripheral Don Juan, but I had no idea what they were chattering about. Then I decided to seek revenge and pretended that I had fallen asleep. I was 'brought back to my senses' by a slight jolt. The Mermaid was standing over me, laughing:

"My God, how uncouth he really is. He's asleep!"

"Who?" I asked irritably and, to enhance the effect, looked askance at Borys. He was smugly and knowingly grinning.

"Let's go for a swim," the Mermaid invited me meekly.

I got to my feet without saying a word and traipsed after her to the banks of the Dnipro River.

II

A few days later I was terribly surprised to receive a letter.

Serhiy, my dear! I bet you never expected to receive this message. I bet this epistle will be completely unexpected and will possibly give you grounds to suspect that I'm hounding you. Who cares…! You were already so sure that I would never find out who you were, and yet the opposite has happened. Your loquacious countryman told me everything. I even know that in school you both had the hots for the same girl, and that she chose him. And she was right to do so — you're so stupid and thick, or maybe just malicious? If you have any conscience at all, drop by or write.

Zina the Mermaid.

There followed an address and the author's personal particulars, followed by this snippet of information: '*Our doorbell doesn't work — you need to knock.*'

I liked the tone and style of the letter. I tried to be as subdued and upbeat as I could with my answer.

Darling Mermaid! I am no fan of epistolary creativity, but I take my hat off to you — you're a natural. I might have even fallen in love with you, had you been five years younger. But unfortunately, it's not often you get to meet twenty-year-old actresses. By the way, your childlike spontaneity is rather cute, it suits you.

Ringing doorbells or knocking on doors is not my style. I'm much too lazy. See ya.

Fisherman.

The reply came back straight away.

I received your insolent letter yesterday and hung around the university for half a day to slap the face of its impudent author. But you deftly managed to avoid your just desserts. Think I didn't see you sneak into the trolleybus? I'm not that retarded, not to guess to get in the next one and to head for the railway station. Pity that the train left right in front of my nose.

Only someone like you would be capable of imagining, that I'm all of twenty-five years old — actually, I'm only eighteen. You can come and check my birth certificate. By the way, the doorbell's been fixed.

Your friend Borys is a cad. He sent me a maudlin abstract about my beauty and assures me that I am sweet, as if I were laced with honey.

Mermaid.

This was a little too much. I boiled over with anger and spite. I wrote back an angry, but convoluted letter. Here are my ramblings:

Esteemed miss! I'm sick and tired of your stories, and I want to put an end to them. I won't deny that you played the childish role in this comedy marvellously, but enough is enough. The curtain is falling. I'm not that stupid and short-sighted to let cute dolls play with me. If you still have at least some semblance of decency and shame, then leave me in peace. Don't even think of writing back — I won't be reading the letter or answering it.

III

I live in a small worker's settlement near Kyiv. There is none of that meaningless urban bustle here, but absent also is that sleepy rural calm. A pine forest rustles away here in the evenings, and the uneasy whistles of the steam engines don't upset its grand indifference. I love listening to its murmur, but it holds no magic for me — it is monotonous, dignified, and haughty. I venture deeper, into the gullies, where centuries-old oaks hallucinate as if in a dream, where aspens quarrel senselessly, and the maples — hopeless pessimists that they are — sigh after their long-lost youth. This is my one and only consolation and luxury.

I have no friends, whom I could love unconditionally and whom I could trust implicitly. I don't despise people, but for some reason I try to keep to myself. This is probably because I can see through people. I want people to be happy, but for this they must first be intelligent.

Today I was in for a surprise in the woods. Some weirdos dressed in ancient baggy Cossack pants, embroidered overcoats and black and grey tall sheepskin hats scrambled about in the gully, rolling prehistoric cannons here and there, making an incredible racket. Dozens of gawkers were perched in the trees, hundreds of people stood in a tight circle around the gully.

I had no desire to return home and began to mingle with these excited layabouts. As I made my way down to the dam, I was stopped by a zany spectre dressed in old-fashioned clothes.

"I knew I'd meet you again. Recognize me?"

"Mermaid! Why are you decked out in those rags?"

"Can't you see – they're shooting a film."

"Ah, I forgot. You're an actress."

"I'm not really an actress. It's just that my mum's sick and so I perform in the crowd scenes. I was just showing off back then. Why have you got it out for me?"

"Still hasn't sunk in?"

61

"I detest you, Fisherman! I feel like giving you a good hiding."

"Try."

"I feel a little sorry for you," sighed the beauty from the Middle Ages. "If only you knew how much your phlegmatism irritates me!"

"I can relieve you of my presence."

"No, that's not to be. They're finishing shooting, and I won't leave your side until you explain everything down to the last detail."

"What's there to explain?"

"Why you're so mad at me?"

"I was simply irritated and probably wrote more than I should have. Did I offend you?"

"No, I was pleased."

"So, what more do you want?"

"I'll go and change in a flash. Wait for me. I'll be quick."

"I won't wait."

"Then I'll come round to your place!"

"I may not be there."

"You'll have to come back some time. I'll be waiting!"

"All right, then. Go and change."

Why was I carrying on like that then? I get annoyed now just remembering it.

We wandered through the forest for a long time. Mermaid spoke so much, that only a massive computer could have remembered everything.

It was after midnight when we finally came to our senses and raced off to catch the train. We must have been the only people in our carriage. The sleepy conductor threw us spiteful glances, but it had no effect on either Mermaid or me.

The city slept an enchanted electrical sleep. We made our way along empty streets, and when the vaults of bridges rose above us, it seemed as if we were deep in the catacombs. Zina then squeezed my hand more strongly and whispered:

"The riff-raff hang out here. Aren't you afraid?"

Soon we indeed came across some nurslings of the dark night. A morose young fellow loutishly asked me for a cigarette. He deeply breathed in the smoke, spat with a flourish, and declared calmly:

"Such a young gal, and already working the streets."

"You're a cretin!" I exclaimed unexpectedly as blood rushed into my temples.

"Oh! It appears you're swearing. That's impolite. As a first-time offender we can let you off in your underpants."

I noticed that two more figures were approaching us from behind.

"Out of my way," I took a step toward the grateful smoker. "Move, I said!"

He calmly took out a bowie knife and strained the words through his teeth, not without a hint of contempt: "Take off your clothes. You too, mademoiselle…"

I must have really taken fright, because only now did I remember that Zina was with me. No, I couldn't let them disgrace me that easily! I was pretty good at boxing, and in a flash the stepchild of the night fell to the asphalt with a bloodied nose. I grabbed Zina by the hand:

"Run, stupid!"

Poor Mermaid could barely move her feet. We ran off some thirty metres or so, while our benefactors were regaining their senses. Behind us I heard threats, liberally interspersed with emotional swearing.

But we had won enough time. Zina finally realized what was expected of her and fear gave her so much strength that I could barely keep up with her. The riffraff had stopped chasing us because we had run out onto a well-lit street.

We walked along not uttering a word, until we caught our breaths. Zina was white, her hands were shaking, but she regained her talkativeness.

"That was a stunning punch. I didn't even realize how you did it. Were you scared? There must have been a dozen of them."

"There were only three."

"Really? But it seemed to me... no matter... You'll have to go to the railway station another way now. I'll show you how."

"There's no point in going to the railway station. The last train left half an hour ago."

"Well, then stay the night at our place. Really, why didn't I think of that before?"

"Stop talking rubbish. You know full well that I won't do that."

"Fool! And why's that?"

"Simply because it's not nice."

"So what? You weren't afraid of the riff-raff, d'you think it's more dangerous to sleep in the same room as me?"

She herself realized the absurdity of the question. We burst out laughing and slowed our pace. We kept walking the streets until morning.

IV

I became completely possessed by Zina. I no longer viewed her with disdain and continually found excuses to pop in to see her for a minute or two. These excuses were naïve and foolish, but she believed with a childish sincerity, that I couldn't take a step without her advice. And by the way, she wasn't far wrong.

Zina was a sweet child, frank, easy-going, and she was only insincere when she devotedly tried to be angry with me. She was especially irritated by my nihilism. She was the one who usually began these conversations.

"You once said," she recalled, biting on her small puffy lip, "that brutality is always criminal. But what if it's in the name of future good?"

"See, Mermaid," I replied profoundly, "where there is a hint of blood, the happiness and joy of others reminds me of the barbaric bacchanalia over sacked Rome and Greece. The barbarians destroyed slavery for the future good, but they didn't spare the richness of the culture either. Because of their actions people remained savages and cretins for a whole millennium. This was an unwise path to take. People need to find other ways. That's what Lenin's life was about."

"But Lenin could be brutal too."

"That's a lie!" I yelled. "He was ruthless, not brutal. And that's natural — truth is always ruthless. No, there's no blood on his hands."

"What about the revolution, the civil war?"

"He didn't kill anyone," I stubbornly insisted. "He only tossed foul-smelling carcasses into the grave."

"You're really good at talking your way out of these things," complained Mermaid. "I can't do that. But what do you want?

"I simply don't want my life to be dependent on the abilities of some tightrope-walking diplomat suspended over an abyss. They've grown fat and at any moment they can drop into the void. And then atom bombs will start exploding. That's frightening."

"You're a smart arse," my opponent reproached me. "But I love you, even though you're tedious and harebrained."

This logic seemed to me to be more sensible than the most stringent conclusions of some of the world's brilliant thinkers. I'm ashamed to recall how ostentatiously wise I had been back then.

Two months later, while I was undertaking practical workplace experience, Zina sent me a letter:

Serhiy dear, I'm very bored without you, there's no one to even argue with. My mum is undergoing treatment in Kislovodsk, and I'm home alone, and I feel frightened because something unfathomable is happening. First and foremost, your friend Borys, who has already managed to find work here, is getting to me with his persistence. He's a dickhead and an egotist. What does he have against you?

I would have dealt with him, but another calamity has occurred. You still probably haven't forgotten those criminals who wanted to undress us under the bridge? Their leader Pendulum (you smashed his nose up pretty badly) recognized me in the street, and this is where it all began. Serhiy dear, he wants me to become his mistress, and says that he'll kill you, if I didn't agree. I told him to not even think about you if he was expecting me to agree. I couldn't think of anything else to say. He's beyond the arm of the militia, who've been hunting him several years now.

Serhiy dear, I'm not afraid of anything and am ready to die rather than belong to someone else. Come back — and we'll get married. Because you're not afraid of anything either, right?

If only you knew how much I love you, you'd come back here and we'd kill this criminal or die in the process, like Romeo and Juliette. Just don't call me a fool for asking you to kiss this sheet of paper, because I've kissed it. You're so kind and you won't get angry at your crazy Mermaid, right?

At the time I didn't realize how serious this was and thought that Mermaid was exaggerating, as usual. I wrote her a jolly letter in reply, then calmly waited for my practical to end and returned to Kyiv in early September.

Zina met me at the railway station and reproached me for a long time about being indifferent and laid-back.

"He's tormenting me! He's threatened to come round to my place tonight again and I'm sure he'll repeat his threats. I'm afraid."

"If it's really so scary, then we won't bump into him. I'll get a taxi and we can drive right up to your apartment block."

"But taxis are incredibly expensive…"

"Stupid, do you think I have something more precious to protect than the good mood of my little Mermaid?"

Zina gratefully squeezed my hand and sighed.

"You're such a liar, Fisherman! Can you see him over there by the kiosk? Smoking a cigarette. I told you he'd be waiting for us."

After we drove off some fifty metres, I asked the driver to stop the car.

"Wait for me here ten minutes or so."

"Where are you off to?" Zina wouldn't let go of my hand. I could feel she was trembling.

"I'll just say hello to Pendulum. Don't worry, everything will be fine," and I forcefully extricated my hand from hers, lit a cigarette and went off to face my adversary. "Hi, there, Pendulum. How's that nose of yours? I once had the good fortune to stroke it. I hope you'll continue to let me enjoy this small luxury. Recognize me?"

Pendulum was taken aback somewhat by my arrogance, but he replied guardedly:

"Yeah, I remember. It was quite some punch you threw. But you've obviously not come here to apologize, right?"

"Correct. I've simply come to tell you not to stand about here anymore. Zina is my wife."

"That's a lie!" Pendulum spat out his cigarette and repeated: "That's a lie! She'd never do that. She knows what I'm like."

"Quit bragging, Pendulum. Your card's been trumped. And if you refuse to accept this, then I'll be forced to finish you off too."

"Crackpot, and how will you do that?"

"That's my business. But for now — goodbye. My wife's waiting for me," and I headed for the taxi.

"I was so terribly worried," Zina whispered in between our kisses and her tears. "You're so reckless and you don't show me any pity. What did you tell him?"

"Nothing much, I just lied that you were already my wife."

"He'll kill us, Serhiy, he will. But before that I'll become yours."

Staggering, Mermaid came up to the window and drew the curtain closed.

"Don't think that I'm being brash. But I'm not about to keep my virginity for some rapist?"

She rushed up to me, sobbing, and reproached herself for being indecisive.

V

For a while Pendulum stopped pursuing her, and we began to forget about his existence. But in October Zina received a letter from him, which was essentially addressed to me.

Mademoiselle! Have you not yet tired of that insane bar-room brawler? Let him know that my patience is wearing thin. I want to speak to him right away. I'm a noble man and don't like to resolve conflicts based on love by stabbing people in the back. Have him appear at midnight the day after tomorrow under the bridge where we first met. I'll have two of my boys with me as back-up. He can bring along a few friends as well. Be warned: in the event of any provocation I won't pussy-foot around. Mademoiselle, I hope you have a high regard for my patience and my feelings toward you.

Zina used every ounce of influence she had over me to stop me from meeting with the fellow. But I didn't want the lowlife to think that I was a coward. Then she delivered an ultimatum: I had to at least take Borys along with me. To which I was forced to agree.

And here we were under the bridge. I moved away from Borys, clenched my fists, and approached Pendulum. He was standing there and smoking. Behind him two shadows were leaning against a column.

"You came?" Pendulum said calmly. "I hope you've grown a little wiser and we can come to an agreement here."

"That depends on you," I lit up, in an attempt to hide my agitation.

"Alright, first thing's first, you have to pass Zina over to me."

"Let's first agree, that this will never happen," I mechanically corrected him.

"Not bad," Pendulum smiled. "Some of my lads could take a lesson from you. But I don't need any of this stuff."

"Listen, Pendulum, you're an out-and-out crim. But we're not here to exchange compliments."

"You're no fool and no coward," Pendulum again bared his teeth. "But I'll be forced to give you a leg-up into heaven, if you remain so stubborn."

"That won't be so easy, Pendulum," I sympathized with him.

"Don't think that there's just the three of us. I know what you're like, so I've posted an extra two lads on either side of the bridge. You did well to bring that whipper-snapper with you. He can go call the militia so that your body doesn't lie here till morning."

"So, I'm trapped then?"

Pendulum nodded graciously.

"Thanks for your frankness. Then I'll have to play the game by your rules," I moved closer and offered him my hand, but at that moment I felled the wretch with two blows to his stunned mug and neck.

After that all hell broke loose before my eyes. I heard screaming, people swearing, and that was the last thing that was imprinted on my memory. Later, when I was lying in hospital with a hole between my ribs, the investigator told me that Zina had brought the militia just in time, and he also said that I was a donkey and that I had learnt very little in life.

VI

From the hospital I was passed into the arms of a Mykola Vynokur. Obviously, he was a good person, but it would have been better had I never made his acquaintance. He spent a long time checking me out thoroughly, turning my soul inside out like a pocket, and I don't know if he found any sustenance there.

I couldn't stand this and said one day:

"What are you after? Is it such a big crime that I never notified anyone about my rendezvous with Pendulum?"

He eyed me with an obviously sympathetic look, swore and sang out in his chamber-choir tenor:

"What am I after? My hands are itching to throw you out of here."

"Then who's stopping you, for God's sake!"

He looked at me once more, as if I were an utter idiot, and asked unexpectedly:

"Do you have any enemies?"

"No."

"None at all?"

I rummaged about in my memory a little.

"If you're referring to personal enemies, then I really don't have any. Apart from Pendulum, of course."

For a long-long time he drilled those angry grey eyes of his into me, then took a scrap of paper out of a drawer and intoned, before pressing it into my hands:

"I wonder which of your friends wrote this?"

I began to devour what someone had clapped out there on a typewriter, and my head began to spin. Some scoundrel had written that I had 'found a "mistake" in Marxism' and was now looking for a way to hot-foot it abroad. Pendulum had allegedly agreed to give me a helping hand, but at the last minute we had supposedly quarrelled over a mistress. It also stated there that I had a zoological hatred of the Soviet system and had even tried to set up an underground cell.

I couldn't help myself and burst out laughing. The investigator snatched the denunciation from me and tossed it back into the drawer.

"Calm down there, you donkey!"

"Do you believe there's even a grain of truth in there?"

"I'm the one asking the questions here!" he shouted, then added in a more conciliatory tone:

"If I did, I wouldn't have shown it to you. And by the way, you never saw that bit of dirt," he nodded in the direction of the drawer.

He remained silent for a long time, then complained:

"You've gotten under my skin. This isn't an investigation, it's god only knows what. I don't need to prove your guilt. I don't have and never will have any evidence apart from that bit of shit. But you... do you have any proof, that you're not guilty?"

"But that's obvious!"

"You're too smart, lad. You didn't try to create an underground cell? Where's the evidence, where are the witnesses, that you're telling the truth? Can you find people who will testify that you never entertained any thoughts about escaping abroad?"

"But you can accuse any old person of such things!"

"We're not talking about any old person here, but about you."

"Everyone knows me in class..."

Vynokur grimaced contemptuously and waved his arm:

"I've spoken with your fellow classmates. They all say you're secretive and keep to yourself. Only one fellow — Victor... what's his name... the one who lives with you, declared straight out: 'Serhiy is an honest lad, even though he has his quirks...' He put together a petition, tried to get people to sign it, but no one wanted to listen to him."

He was silent again for a long time, and meanwhile my head was spinning: what could I answer back?

"What happened to your grandpa?" he suddenly intruded into my thoughts. I flinched.

"Grandpa was taken away in thirty-seven. No one can say why. He was a communist from 1913. Father was executed by the Germans. He'd been a partisan."

I don't know why, but I suddenly could not hold back. I told him everything about myself and my mother, and mentioned that my arrest would be the end of her.

"Write her that I was sent off somewhere... I mean, on an assignment... somewhere far away... or with a delegation... Anything, but the truth..."

I suddenly began to snivel like a schoolkid, tears poured from my eyes like water from a dripping tap. I sat and sobbed, unable to control myself, my whole body in convulsions. The devil take whoever dreamed up tears and all that stuff! Had I been born in an incubator, like a chick, I'd be able to live like green grass, not thinking about anyone, and there would be no one to worry about me.

Maybe it only seemed that way to me, but I felt that Vynokur nearly shed a tear too. He moved away to a corner and stood there with his back to me. Or maybe he was simply disgusted to watch such a bull of a man snivelling away.

Finally, he turned around to face me and said:

"That's enough. Shame on you. Go and rest."

I was led off to my cell.

The next day he told me the most frightening news:

"We need to rescue you. It's too late to save your mother."

I flinched, as if scalded, and looked imploringly into his eyes. He lowered his head and almost whispered:

"Yes. Her heart broke when she found out... Victor wrote to her. This happened a week ago."

"And I wasn't even allowed to... attend the funeral?"

He was awfully pale. Like death warmed up. He couldn't even look in my general direction, let alone look me in the eye. Was he to blame? It was that scum which put that dirty scrap of paper into the typewriter which had killed my mother. And maybe even my grandpa? Who knows, maybe it was that very same damned hatchling from a rotten egg who had dobbed in my father too?

"A shard of her heart is sticking out of my chest," I could hear the distant tenor of Mykola Vynokur. "I'll hang myself if I don't extricate you from this mess."

'Hang myself — now that was a good idea. Thanks for suggesting it,' I thought, but out loud I said something quite different:

"I don't care what happens now."

Then for some two weeks I was interrogated by a desiccated fellow with a head which looked like a billiard ball. He set up so many traps for me, that I was saved only because I had nothing to hide. I wanted to ask what had happened to Vynokur but stopped short. Why cast a shadow on a good man?

After I had been freed, I learnt that Vynokur had gone to Moscow because of me to meet with some bigwig. I was released only after some bastard of a minister was arrested. Pity they only arrested one.

Victor was waiting for me when I was released, together with a letter from Zina. She wrote that I was scum and she'd rather swallow cactuses that spend time with me. May you choke on your words! You traitor!

In my class at university everyone became so courteous and polite, that I wanted to puke…

I am sitting in the kitchen at an unpropitious table and as I write it creaks in time to my movements. Spring nights are short, especially when it's the last night of one's life.

There's a rope in my drawer. In a few minutes I will take it from there and leave this letter in its place. 'Who needs my life if I myself have no need of it? I've tired of everything.'

VII

I looked away from the papers and looked at Borys.

"Life wasn't too sweet for this poser, but what do you have to do with all this?"

He pulled out another incredibly tattered sheet of paper from his pocket and wordlessly offered it to me.

You snake! I read there. Remember how you came to me in the evening and said: 'Serhiy's been transferred from the hospital to the prison…' — 'Why?' I shuddered. 'We never knew who he really was, Zina,' you pretended to be upset. 'He was someone quite different…' 'What did he do? Tell me and don't keep me in suspense!' You hummed and hawed for a long time and then delivered a blow to my heart: 'For debauchery and thuggery. He's a friend of Pendulum's. All those 'clashes' were just a ploy to get you to be his… He had countless others like you…' I was racked by fever, I cried terribly and cursed you for lying to me, but you… you were 'visiting' the investigator, 'chatting' with the prosecutor, and finally you 'met' with Serhiy. — 'Serhiy didn't even want to talk with me. I asked: 'What should I tell Zina?' 'Tell her,' he laughed, 'that in my harem I relegated her to third place. She should be proud of that,' did you not say that, you louse?

What made me believe you? My Lord, what a wretch I am! Mykola Vynokur came to see me today — he's the investigator who conducted Serhiy's case. He was utterly gobsmacked when he learned why I had broken off with Serhiy.

You miserable conniving bastard! You wanted me to feel something for you. Well, you've reached your goal: I detest you!

I'm going to Serhiy and I'll crawl before him on all fours until he forgives me, the idiot that I am. But you… If you are still in Kyiv tomorrow, then the day after will be your funeral. Vynokur said that he would conduct the investigation and would make sure it was wound up.

I hate you! I hate you! I hate you!

I studied the letter, as if wanting to read something which was not there.

Only after the silence became explosive, did I ask fiercely:

"So, you were the one who wrote the anonymous note denouncing him?"

He grimaced and seemed to croak:

"Serhiy was about to hang himself when you and Zina broke into his place…"

"You want to restore his faith in people?"

He nodded and it seemed to me that his ears were moving.

"What made you think that he lost faith in people?" With this question I felled him at close range. "He was getting the noose ready because he had lost faith in himself."

74

He dilly-dallied and was probably thinking hard of something to say, because I could hear his brain creaking away. In fact, it was only his chair.

"You know," Borys said, 'one can't torment oneself all one's life. This happened only because of Zina. Right now, I couldn't care less about her, but I still like Serhiy the way I used to…"

I burst out laughing in disbelief.

"I know it sounds funny," Borys continued, "but I really do love him."

"Then go and make peace with him."

"Maybe Serhiy doesn't even suspect, that I am to blame for his woes. But Zina… She'll throw me out. Perhaps you could have a chat with her and find out if she told him…"

"Listen, Borys," I replied, "tell me honestly, what is it you want from me?"

He squirmed once more for a while, searching for the right words, as if he were seeking the end of some thread in a cocoon.

"I'm sick and tired of living in some backwater. I want to be in the thick of things. Yes, I'm to blame. But…"

"In other words, you want to be sure that Serhiy will keep his mouth shut, if you return to Kyiv?"

He kept endlessly studying the parquetry floor. Then I heard a barely audible 'yes'.

"Then why all this melodrama with the repentance. It's unlikely Serhiy will want to sully his hands with you," I said and very much wanted to turn public prosecutor. "In general, you'd do better to remain in your little neck of the woods. Serhiy may feel disgust, but Zina and I… We'll never forget how we pulled him out of that noose. I'll yell at the top of my voice at every intersection that you're a snake…"

He grabbed his jacket and made a run for it, while I yelled after him like some madman:

"I'll go about everywhere and scream: 'Good people! There's a snake crawling in your midst. Don't ever trust him again!'"

It seemed as if the trolleybus into which he dived under my window grimaced in disgust.

1956-1962

The One-Armed Forester

He returned from the war with a Party card, four medals and twenty ribs. After the drums had stopped beating in the house and the ancient accordion had run out of breath, and the guests had drunken and eaten everything the war had not managed to swallow up, and had left, Petro said to his mother:

"Tell Motrya that she should get married..."

His mother clapped her overworked hands together:

"But she's been waiting for you all this time, as if you were God Himself!"

"What of it? Tell her to get married," he repeated with a voice brimming with gloomy disappointment and astringent bitterness.

"You think she doesn't know... the state you're in?" his mother almost sobbed. "That warm grey turtledove loves you all the same..."

"No, mum," the son brutally cut her short. "I won't hear of it."

Motrya dashed in the next day. Her large eyes, filled with grief and insult, looked into his blue ice-chests and she asked:

"Why, my love, why? Don't marry me then, only don't loathe me, as if I was some damned bitch."

"I don't loathe you, Motrya. It's just that..."

"Then let's simply be friends..."

"That's impossible," he forced the words stiffly from his mouth, staring into space somewhere past her.

"But why? Tell me why?"

"It's impossible," he replied, clenching his only fist. "It's utterly impossible, because I love you..."

Their conversation was lengthy, weighty, and depressing. At midday, the teacher walked away with her burden of troubles and undeserved shame, moving past inquisitive dull windows facing the street. She wept as she went, without bothering to hide her tears.

And three days later another bombshell struck the village. Petro came to the office of the village council and said to the chairman:

"Give me a job."

"Come on, lad," the fellow practically recoiled. "You're a teacher, we haven't got anyone to teach the children how to write properly."

"I won't work in the school!"

"The Lord preserve you, Petro," the old chairman said, rising from his ancient stool. "Why don't you want to teach?"

Petro stared past him with terrifying empty eyes. His jaws were tightly clenched, and it looked as if they would crack at any moment.

"I hate children," he groaned. "I don't want to teach in the school. If you're a real man, appoint me as the forester. Because I can only find a common language with the she-wolves." And he suddenly burst into almost hysterical sobs and squatted faintly onto the bench against the wall.

Petro became a forester. He shied away from everyone, especially the youngsters, and lived and slept in the forest. And although he became a very able forester, everyone in the village was afraid of him. Some said that during the war he had lost more than his arm, he'd also lost his marbles. Others said that it wasn't his ribs that had been removed, but his heart.

Petro didn't listen to this twaddle. He was completely engrossed in forestry matters and only dealt with people when his job necessitated it. In two years, he had replanted nearly all the collective farm's barren clearings and gullies with oaks, maples, lindens, and willows.

Who knows what had brought them together, him and old man Omelko, the one everyone in the village had nicknamed Kheteze? Possibly because he had received four death notices from the front, the old man began to shun people and even avoided appearing at home, where his half-dead wife wasted away. The one-armed chimera and mangy old Kheteze, scoured by age and insufferable grief, roamed the village and the forest like two enamoured apparitions. Whether they ever spoke to each other – no one could say for sure with a clear conscience. Maybe they did, maybe they didn't.

However, after Petro and the old man had a glass or two of alcohol, hordes of children would gather around them. The old man became a veritable factory. In no time at all he was able to supply the silly barefoot fools with linden whistles, hazel-wood trumpets, elder-wood popguns, and annoying rattles. Then the children whistled, trumpeted, chirred, and rattled away in every house. The mothers did not know whether to thank the old man or to curse him.

While old Kheteze was thus engaged, Petro told the kids such enchanting stories and tales, that they no longer noticed the merciless mosquitoes biting them. But the intoxication wore off and everything returned to its boring grey state. Once again something inexplicable drove them away from human conversation, laughter and song, and they rummaged about the forest like doomed souls, looking for something to do, or possibly sought out herbs to assuage their crucified hearts.

I was only a nipper then, but I can still clearly recall the taste of acorn bread and pancakes leavened on bran and young linden leaves. That frightful spring hunger did not pass by a single honest household in our village[5]. When the harvest began, we ran over the stubble with our reed baskets, collecting wheat-ears, rubbing them between our hands, extracting golden grains of wheat. Emaciated mothers would then grind the grains into handfuls of flour and treated us to improbable flat cakes in the morning.

But one evening mother told me:

"A fatso in underpants has arrived from the centre. He's telling people to stop collecting the wheat-ears or they'll be prosecuted. So, don't go into the fields tomorrow, Hryshka. Let them choke on those awns."

---

[5] Reference to the forced famine of 1930-33, when millions of Ukrainian peasants died.

79

But how could we stop collecting the wheat-ears. We wanted to eat. And we ventured out into the fields. Everything went well, but then just before noon the patrolman Pryvitny came across us. The older lads managed to dash off into the gully, but he blocked my way with his stallion and swore:

"Come on, you little bastard, off to the village council with you. We'll find out whose son you are and put some sense into your mother."

Swearing and cracking his whip, he drove me across the stubble toward the road. I don't remember how long I ran. The stubble stung my bare feet, the sweat poured into my eyes, the basket struck my legs, my body filled with an animal fright and exhaustion. I ran and felt that I would collapse any minute and be unable to get to my feet. The horse wheezed behind me and vulgar curses filled the air.

"What are you doing, you skunk?!" someone's words suddenly burst into my consciousness. I stopped and tore my eyes away from the stubble. There before me was Petro, prancing on his horse, looking so frightening, like some devil.

"I won't a-nee-more, un-cle," I whined. But Petro was oblivious to my plea. He charged past me. I jumped to one side, and as I tripped and fell backwards, I saw him bring the whip down violently on Pryvitny's head.

"You mad or something?" the fellow shrieked. But Petro brought him down off his horse with a second violent lash and continued to flog him at length, savagely and mercilessly. At first Pryvitny called the forester a one-armed Satan, then he pleaded with him to stop and eventually he went completely quiet.

When Petro brought me home I was unconscious. Afterwards, mother took me to all kinds of grannies for over a year to cast the fright out of me. What happened next, I can only recount from the words of others, for the rest of that year I vegetated and little broke through into the secluded corners of my mind.

They wanted to put Petro on trial for cruelly assaulting a person in the performance of their official duty, and for aiding and abetting plunderers of socialist property. But prior to that, they decided to publicly expel him from the Party and the collective farm, as a lesson to others.

The meeting was conducted on the village common for everyone who could walk came along. Women wept, the war cripples wheezed silently, even the teenagers did not get up to their pranks, as they were wont to do.

The head man from the centre, the one in 'underpants', took the bull by the horns straight away:

"Petro Pidoshva must be tried as a criminal. He should be thrown out of the Party lock, stock, and barrel. It's a disgrace that in our exemplary times such degenerates should still exist..."

"Only who's the degenerate?" a voice burst from the crowd and immediately grew silent. The head man gave the anonymous anarchist a fitting rebuke and suggested they hear out Petro.

"What can I say?" Petro began, rising to his feet. "If the Party supports the mistreatment of children, then throw me out. Before I leave of my own accord. I didn't fight for this. I'm missing an arm and I've got four ribs less than other people. The war also killed my unborn children," he uttered the last words in a whisper, but everyone heard. Suddenly Petro turned and called into the agitated crowd:

"Motrya, are you here?"

"I'm here," the girl answered, as if from the other world.

"Then in front of all these people I beg you to forgive me for my injustice. Now you know, why I turned you away..."

He practically collapsed onto the grass and a weighty silence fell with him. The head man in white pants tore it into shreds:

"Playing on your accomplishments? Want to wash away your crimes with a tear? It won't work! We've seen the likes of you! We'll mercilessly sweep away such rubbish from our ranks."

"Bite that tongue of yours," old man Kheteze jumped to his feet. "Let me have a word."

"You're not in the Party, old man, so you've no right to speak..."

81

"So, I've no right? Maybe you want this?!" and he thrust his paltry finger into the air. "I've held four funerals and my sons were all communists. So, I've no right?"

"Let the old man speak! He's held his breath for long enough," the people buzzed.

And the old man continued:

"You can't demote me because there's no lower position than mine. And you won't be able to hurt me because there's no greater misfortune than the one I have suffered. So, listen and don't interrupt. I had four sons: Yakiv, Ivan, Vasyl and Prokip. The people won't let me lie to you. Hitler has orphaned me and now there is no one left to bury me. But then I found myself a fifth son – Petro here. The Germans hadn't quite finished him off, so now our lot have decided to sink their teeth into him," the old man suddenly let fly at the visitor. "Are you worth even his little finger? Perhaps you want to throw my dead sons out of the Party too, you carrion? Eh? Well, you yellow belly? Tell me the truth, or I'll pull down those underpants of yours and whip you with nettles. Since nothing else will get through your thick skull, maybe that will get through your arse!"

It took a lot of placating to calm the old man down. Petro was told to keep his hands to himself, while the white-trousered fellow was asked never to venture into the village again.

Motrya came to Petro's house after the meeting. She is still living with him to this day.

10.06.1962

Balm

Suddenly the pain burst its way into their honeymoon. With his cheek swollen, eyes bleary with powerless despair, he stumbled about the room all night long, unable to find any peace. His jaw seemed to be shattering into a thousand shards. It was a dull, monotonous, unending pain. And the most frightening part was that nothing would stop it. Neither gargles nor lotions helped, not even the most ardent oaths made to stop taking notice of this 'zoological nonsense'.

"Don't worry about it, go back to sleep," he tried to reassure Tonya. "Everything will soon pass."

But nothing passed and the primeval animal pain continued to drive the intellectual being insane. At times he felt like grabbing the iron and simply knocking his teeth out with its nickel-plated cold metal.

"Go on, sleep, baby, sleep," Mykola implored her, as if wanting to have no witness to his suffering.

But his baby would not sleep. Under her six-month-old perm new ideas kept being hatched every few minutes. And then the light would flash on, Mykola saw himself in the mirror and quivered with hatred, while she practised her witchcraft with some new home-made remedy.

"Just try to put this on your tooth. Auntie Nata says it's a balm."

The balm obviously did not help at all and he wanted to feed it there and then to Auntie Nata, who had dreamed up this useless filth.

The pauses between the ticking of the clock's pendulum seemed just a little short of entire millenniums. In this time mighty empires had probably appeared and disappeared from the face of the Earth. In short, Mykola managed to live through all the geological ages, traversing the evolutionary path from bacteria to cognizant being. He was ready to repeat the whole process of evolution a second time, when – at last! – morning rolled out its red hoop from behind the hill.

But Tonya had not yet exhausted her arsenal of home remedies. The more he suffered, the more fertile her imagination became. She was once more in the kitchen cooking up some new concoction. The door to the neighbouring room banged shut and then Mykola heard the landlady yawn loudly and ask:

"What was all that clatter during the night? And the lights going on and off."

"We have a toothache," Tonya replied innocently.

'We,' Mykola thought ironically.

And suddenly the pain stopped. Only his head continued to buzz from the lack of sleep.

"Tonya!" he yelled out, collapsing onto the bed. "Forget about your witchcraft. Our tooth has stopped aching!"

27.11.1962

A Friend of the Family

For three months I sighed and suffered over an individual of the fairer sex. My love for her was so electric, that my friends prophesied a quick and easy death. This really alarmed a colleague at work. He decided at all costs to wrest me from the embrace of the bony reaper and toss me into the arms of a platonic mistress.

"Forget about her," my anxious friend begged me.

I groaned silently and continued to die a protracted death. My colleague wiped his damp eyes with the palm of his hand and made a final attempt to avert my demise.

"Listen, unlucky lover boy," he whispered sympathetically, "let me act on your behalf."

I agreed to this.

My friend began his activity very simply. Each day he would send her my jottings, accompanying them with his own witticisms.

"How are things progressing?" I would ask him every half an hour.

"It's all plain sailing," replied the colleague and asked for some paper to make notes.

Each evening he would present me with a broad overview of events of the previous day, telling me in detail how she blushed at the mention of my name. In a separate notebook he recorded her every sigh and smile.

"Another day or two, and she'll be all yours," my heart's representative assured me, beaming with happiness.

You won't be surprised, of course, if I tell you that several days after this my loved one and my colleague got married. Smitten by grief and weakened by love, I wanted only to die. However, in a flash I had changed my mind and decided to become a close friend of their family. Now we are all in heaven. Although lately my friend has gone completely insane. He keeps threatening to divorce her. Just let him try! At the trade-union meeting – and nothing will come to pass without it! – I will get up and tell everyone the kind of person he is. And I won't even take into account that he's a close friend.

First published in *Sotsialistychna kul'tura*, #12/1988

A Conversation Overheard

Opanas Shvoren knew that all those who loved to moralise were like parrots. Even in antiquity people asserted that it was dishonest to listen in on other people's conversations. That was a long time ago, for even Opanas' grandfather could not recall those times. However, in our times moralists have not tired of repeating these primitive truths.

Opanas Shvoren's grandfather agreed with him, for he had never been a poet. But a person's psychology was truly revealed during intimate conversations, and what poetry was there without a dollop of psychology?

Each evening Shvoren would conceal himself in the thickest bushes of some park and become all ears. Couples in love walked to and fro. They spoke in whispers and mostly nonsense. Before dawn, bitten by mosquitoes, his face scratched all over, Opanas would return home from his quest. Only a lucky incident saved his talent from inevitable demise.

One evening a young couple stopped beside the bush from behind which the talented poet was studying life. The girl was pretty, but heartless, the fellow – dour and frightened.

"Oh, don't devastate me," the lad begged in a snivelling voice.

"Quit grimacing," came the implacable reply.

The lad could not hold back his tears. He tried to get down on his knees, but his legs would not bend.

Overjoyed, Shvoren jumped out of his hide, energetically shook each of their hands and raced off home.

By morning, the poem was ready. When Opanas recited it to the plump check-out lady in the shop, she wept and said:

"Beautiful. Especially the last lines: 'My life is not worth a penny, you've butchered me without a knife.' It has the smell of blood there."

A month later the poem was published in a magazine.

Future events developed at breakneck speed. The heartless beauty thought the author of the poem was none other than her unlucky lover. She immediately returned his love.

"Oh, my Ovid," she pressed herself to his chest.

"What Ovid are you talking about?" the lad looked wide-eyed at her.

"But didn't you write this?" the worshipper of muses opened the magazine.

"No… It's the first time I've seen it…"

"Why, you…"

And she hit him on the bridge of the nose with the heavy periodical.

The female criminal was detained at the inquiry desk, where she was attempting to obtain the address of Opanas Shvoren. And thus, the police rescued his unique talent for posterity.

First published in Sotsialistychna kul'tura, #12/1988

No One Knows

They had nothing to talk about. A white dust devil was dancing about on the balcony, the sky started beyond the balcony, and the world finished here in the room. Seven blind elephants stood on a sideboard guarding the serenity of the apartment.

He came home from work, fastidiously wiped his shoes on the rubber mat and asked:

"Where's Borya?"

"Playing in the yard."

Then he sat on the sofa, opened the newspaper, and lit a cigarette. At times she added:

"Borya's become really malicious. Today he beat up little Valeriy.

"Why?"

"Because he broke Ihor's toy car."

"Valeriy's always picking on smaller kids. Borya was right to do what he did."

"But you should have heard the hoo-ha Zina raised…"

(Valeriy and Ihor were the neighbour's children. They were friends with Borya, even though they exchanged punches almost every day… They quarrelled three times each minute and then chanted three times each minute: 'Peace, forever peace. He who quarrels is a pig!" They quarrelled again and made up again, meanwhile their temperamental mothers, engrossed in domestic affairs, sometimes stopped talking to one another for several weeks on end because of this.)

Silence filled the room. A white dust devil danced about on the balcony, and fluff from the poplars adhered to the white curtains.

Long ago they had said everything that they had to say to one another. Actually, they only had something to talk about the first two to three years. Then Olha noticed that Petro was no longer interested in listening to her accounts of domestic preoccupation, and Petro noticed that Olha began to yawn when he told her about his woes on construction sites. By silent agreement they stopped talking about these things, and it turned out that in fact they had nothing left to share.

Often, he would arrive as the darkness of evening was falling. Gulping down some cold beetroot soup, he heard her lying silently in bed. Then came the feigned sleepy words:

"Where were you so long?"

"We had a delivery of cement today."

Silence once more, and again the sleepy voice:

"Just after we got married, they delivered cement far less often…"

"Back then we were just building a workshop, and now we're building a whole factory. And back then I had dozens of workers under me, while now I have hundreds to deal with."

"There were simply less girls back then."

"Yes. And you also had less time to give reign to your imagination…"

"Mum, if you worked in the factory, you'd be coming home late too. You don't know how great it is there!" Borya suddenly piped up.

"It's way past your bedtime!" she put him in his place. "Eggs don't preach to chickens!"

"No one preaches to chickens," our son snapped back.

"Borya!" This time it was his father. That meant that he was out of line.

One time, after a similar exchange, Petro asked:

"How can you live and not aspire to anything?"

She was terribly offended.

"What do you mean, not aspire to anything? I'm trying to protect our family."

"From whom?"

Having nothing more to say in reply, she used the most persuasive feminine ploy there was — tears. He felt sorry for Olha and said:

"But that can't be a purpose in life. A family doesn't need to be protected if it's real."

Olha was terribly unhappy. He had made her that way. And Petro bore the burden of his thirty-two years, his factory, and his guilt before her. He trod heavily, and the earth sank deeply under his feet. He moved among people, he argued, and enjoyed life with them, and this had probably made his hair start to turn grey. He felt like a dust particle in a white dust devil.

He knew that he was loved. But he also knew that he had made one person unhappy. And this was the person whom he had dreamed to make the happiest person in the world. The mere thought of this made him hunch his broad shoulders, and made his steps heavier.

'At which point did I lose Olha?' this spike always protruded from his heart. And Petro did not know how to extract it from there. He loved the Olha who had existed earlier. But the one that he himself had created – he could never understand her. He made her a gift of a beautiful shopping bag and then drove her life into that bag.

He moved about the construction site, personable and friendly. Goodwill and love pursued him everywhere. He had given these people and these walls his charm, and maybe even the beauty he had purloined from Olha.

"Good morning!" people greeted him.

'And none of them know that I'm a criminal,' he thought, and his shoulders became more hunched, and his hair grew greyer, his steps heavier, and sadness lurked in the corners of his eyes and the wrinkles on his forehead.

1.3.1962

My Student Years

A week before my departure I was relieved of all duties around the house. Mother tried to keep me close to her as much as possible and occasionally cried when she thought I couldn't see. But I had itchy feet, I wanted to go somewhere far away into the unknown. Dashing off to the village clubhouse, I pranced about doing the *hopak*, danced the 'apple' and various polkas *ad nauseum*. At night I scribbled rhymes and gave free rein to my imagination.

For days on end my friend Hrysha and I disappeared down by the river. We would return just before sunset, hungry and exhausted, but refreshed and enthusiastic. We would be walking along in complete silence, supporting ourselves with oars, jumping over ditches and pools. Neither of us liked to repeat ourselves and the days were long. We entered the chicken pen and looked for eggs under the hemp plants. Then we began to have fun, tossing them at each other's head. The duel took place according to strict rules. Whoever ducked first was the loser.

Then followed parties in the evening, laughter, more laughter, dancing, and the accordion. And after all this I would stand next to Mariyka's gate and tell her stories about the constellations. Everyone thought I was 'keen on her', but I was simply settling affairs of the heart for my bosom buddy. I have no idea, whether Mariyka realized this.

And several days later our house filled with commotion – people came to see me off, bringing along bottles stuffed with corncobs. The smell of bootleg vodka pervaded the air, people were drawn to song – and things went into a spin. Everyone envied me a little and at the same time they pitied me. Their respect and love for me was expressed in their desire that I down a glass of spirits poured by them personally, and I obliged them. I drank and somehow remained sober. Obviously, I was nervous. Then we went about the village, yelling and chattering away, teasing the dogs and kissing girls goodbye.

Hrysha kept a tight hold of me. Probably because he could not walk on his own two feet. And my cousin Alyosha[6] – a hulk of a guy and an extremely strong fellow – playfully pulled fence posts out of the ground and smashed them in a business-like fashion against telephone poles. Actually, I was more worried that in a sudden display of affection he might want to embrace me. I was afraid, not because I had no faith in doctors, just that I didn't want to set off for the capital Kyiv with broken ribs.

Everything was as if in a dream.

* * *

A day later I got off the Kharkiv train at Kyiv Railway Station. Up until then I had never believed that a person (especially myself) could become so hopelessly lost in a crowd. In the village I had learnt to remember every new face. But here there was such a sea of faces, that I soon had a splitting headache.

I entered the university carrying a large wooden suitcase, valiantly withstanding the doorman's contemptuous gaze. I remember the first friendship I struck up. A young fellow came up to me – for some reason I took him for a senior student – and said very unceremoniously, with a hint of arrogance:

"Greetings, brother! Come to university?"

His gestures were jerky and nervous.

"Aha. Greetings!"

"Which faculty?"

"Philology."

"Ah, a colleague! Which department?"

"Journalism."

"Bosom buddy! And which year?"

"Well, first year," I blurted out mechanically by now.

---

[6] Oleksiy Shcherban, who also wrote poems.

There followed several heartfelt exclamations, an attempt at embracing me and a long, pompous tirade, from which I understood that the 'bosom buddy' still wasn't sure whether he had been accepted into university.

"Do you write poems?" the bosom buddy suddenly asked in Russian. "Yeah, I forgot to introduce myself – Vladimir."

"Vasyl. I've written a poem or two. And you?"

"Of course! I made a fool of myself in literature," he continued in Russian.

This was V. Krinko, my future fellow classmate, a poet who was actually funnier than he was interesting. These self-deprecating words of his were the first and last ones which I heard him utter. Later, he only boasted, although awkwardly and stupidly.

* * *

Room forty-four, to which I was assigned, turned out to be occupied. So, the superintendent squeezed me into room fifty.

"Stay here a few days. Then we'll move you elsewhere."

I was afraid to contradict him. In the evening all my room mates assembled – there were about a dozen of them. It turned out all were litterateurs. Volodymyr, whom I had already met, opened a notebook as thick as a Bible and began to yell out poems with pathos. His namesake, a playwright, rambled on about his connections with writers and savoured his own plays. Vania, a tall and thin fellow, and an even greater 'hick' than me, read his epistle to President Trumann, challenging the fellow to a duel. Everyone was enthusiastic, yelling out, trying to prove something.

This spectacle shook me up. I saw that their poems, just like their banter, were worthless. This was clear as day to me. And I realized that my writing was also stupid, except that I hadn't realized this yet, the way they had. That evening I promised myself never to show anyone my poems.

Such was my first step toward civilization.

* * *

94

My acquaintance with the students in my year left me even more anxious. I understood that there would be no frank and easy-going relationships with anyone.

In the evening I dived into bed, buried my face in my pillow and bit my lips to stop myself from crying. Now I was inexorably drawn back to the village. I wanted to drop everything, to dash back home, to go off with Hrysha to collect acorns, to rummage about in the dry autumn leaves, bake potatoes in a fire and chase after girls in the bushes. And in the evenings...

Eh, those autumn evenings in the Poltava backwoods! How I missed them!

* * *

I never did become close friends with anyone in first year. I liked Yacheikin[7], but I was scared of him, since he was a Kievite, after all. And back then we were very different people.

I remembered the two Perepadia brothers fairly well. But only because I didn't like them. [Mykola] Som evoked nothing but contempt in me.

I could only chat more or less openly with 'tiny' Kiporenko. But the only thing we had in common was the saucepan in which we cooked our meals.

All the same I did have some friends. A warm, semi-jovial relationship survived with my former classmate Andriy. We engaged in laid-back banter with Kolomiyets[8]. There was something familiar and endearing about them. But the class as a whole remained distant and alien.

---

[7] Yuri Yacheikin (1933-2013), became a prose writer and humorist. In second year came under fire during the anti-cosmopolitan campaign for reading racist writers such as Mark Twain. Symonenko supported him at a Communist Youth League meeting, where Yuri was being berated, and said that he too had read Twain. For his efforts Vasyl was thrown out of the university dorm, and moved in with the Yacheikin family.

[8] Volodymyr Kolomiyets (1935-2017), became a poet and eventually a Shevchenko Prize winner.

* * *

Second year at university was ill-fated. I became close with Kolomiytseva. Everything turned out somehow straightforward and primitive. It began with poems and finished with kissing. Then there were many disappointments and lots of distress. Her dull attempts at annoying me merely provoked pity in me. At such moments I was overcome by waves of some idiotic kind of tenderness, and for some reason I figured this was love. She was obviously drawn to me because of my rebelliousness and facile pessimism. The love affair ended like a true tragic comedy.

Now it all seems so funny and superfluous.

* * *

Once Kalikhevych sat down beside me by chance. I looked at him askance – I was a little mistrustful of him, somewhat afraid. Oles was an intelligent lad, and what's more important, a unique lad. Even his face, hands, gait, and gestures were unusual and a little strange. At first, I thought that he was 'hamming it up'. Only in year three did I begin to understand him.

We talked about poetry. I showed him two of my poems. Oles praised one of them and berated me over the other. Thus, the stage was set for our acquaintance.

My friendship with him resulted in many good things. We spoke rarely, but I think always frankly. And I soon came to like Oles – both for the fact that he liked my poems, and because of his criticism and his simplistic, somewhat romantic nature.

I awfully liked to hear him speak about love, about people, even when he accused me of non-existent sins.

1952-55

Contemporary literature is the peculiar domain of the blind: the older writers became blinded in the 1920s by an excessively bright flash of light, while the younger ones (my generation) were born blind.

1956

96

Scraps of Thoughts

> *"Reading other people's diaries without*
> *their permission is the height of villainy."*
> *Simpleton Wilson's unknown aphorism*

18.09.1962

I am beginning this diary not because I want to play at being great. What I need is a friend with whom I can share every single one of my doubts. I know of no more loyal and honest a bosom buddy than paper.

Planet Earth has been bearing me along for twenty-eight years around the sun. There are very few wonderful and good things, which I have managed to achieve in this time. However, I have learnt to stay silent and to be vigilant when I should have been screaming out loudly. And what is even more frightening – I have learnt to be insincere.

Lying must be my profession. I have an innate talent for lying. There are three categories of liars: one type lies to obtain moral or material advantage, the second type lies for the sake of lying and the third type serves lying as an artform. They, in fact, invent or conjecture logical ends to truth. These liars, from my liar's perspective, appear to be honourable. They are literature's reserve. Without them life would become boring, without them truth would become scant and dreary, nauseous, and petty. As it is, honorable lies ennoble truth.

Guided by this, I have most often resorted to the third type of lying. People like me are also needed in literature – with our weak thoughts we will fertilize the ground out of which a giant will one day grow. A future Taras [Shevchenko] or [Ivan] Franko. I await him, as a believer awaits the coming of Christ. I believe I will be lucky enough to hear a joyous hosanna in honour of his coming. I only pray that he does not demean us, small unskilled labourers of poetry that we are. For he will grow out of us.

I could have served literature better, had nature not endowed me with a poor musical ear and defective sight. I cannot see all shades of colour and cannot hear all sounds. Music is my torment. I shall never develop enough to be able to deeply fathom it. I shall never attend that festival of hues, from which Saryan returns a happy man. I can't even truly envy the Saryans and Shostakoviches of this world, just as an illiterate person cannot envy Leo Tolstoy. But he can envy his neighbour, who is able to sign his own name.

19.09.1962

Children sometimes unwittingly say great things. I remember: a year ago my young son Oles and I were out walking near the Kazbet Market. Spying the despot's statue, he asked me:

"Daddy, who's that?"

"Stalin."

"For a moment he looked at the statue and asked, as if absent-mindedly:

"Why did he clamber up there?"

That's true, Stalin did not walk up onto the pedestal, people did not place him there, he clambered up there himself – because of treachery and villainy he clambered up bloodily and insolently, like all executioners. This tiger, who subsisted on human flesh, would have died of rage today to learn what a great find his primitive mass-produced statues have become for collectors of scrap metal.

It is frightening when idolization and fame turn to posthumous shame in one's lifetime. It is not in fact fame, but merely a toy for adult children to enjoy. The only ones unable to understand this are those, who are weak in mind and spirit.

27.09.1962

The writer Mykola Vinhranovsky flashed through our city of Cherkasy today. I first met him in 1958. Probably in September, for the following day we sat in a small room he had rented on Kalinin Square[9] and relished some grapes. We almost became close friends, but then followed years of separation. In four years, he had managed to completely forget our meeting. I hadn't. For even back then he had made a profound and strong impression on me. I believed in him from our very first meeting and consider that I was not mistaken.

Be you damned, worthless money! You've turned me into a slave of the newspaper, and I couldn't go with Mykola to Kaniv back then. I had not experienced such personal loss for a long time since there had never really been anyone to lose.

8.10.1962

Three days and a hundred impressions later. Vinhranovsky, Pyanov[10], Kolomiyets and your sinful servant launched a cavalry attack on the cities of Kryvy Rih and Kirovohrad. Although I was unable to read my poems even once before the crowded auditoriums, I was left satisfied. Mykola [Vinhranovsky] is undoubtedly a tribune. The words of his poems burst with passion and ideas. Beside him one's soul becomes deeper.

We argued with Pyanov about my poem "Roses in Mourning"[11]. In my opinion, one can't confuse the Madonna created by artists with the inherently religious Virgin Mary. Hypocrites dressed in the robes of the illustrious Christ and His Mother have become violators of human flesh and spirit. When even the most wonderful legend (and I consider Jesus and the Virgin Mary creations of genius) becomes a means of spiritual oppression, then I can't even

---

[9] Now Independence Square.

[10] Volodymyr Pyanov (1921-1956), literary critic and translator.

[11] Original title of the poem "Damnation" (*Prokliattia*) which Symonenko wrote in a letter to his cousin was about their great-grandfather Trokhym.

begin to judge the 'dramatis personae' of the legend, without reference to what fanatics do, cloaking themselves in these names. No highly honourable and highly obscure edicts of any teaching can serve progress when they become a reference standard. The immaculate Virgin Mary is worthy of eliciting rapture, but, frankly, not emulation. The renunciation of carnal joys is unnatural and therefore cruel and reactionary.

Besides, in my poem "Roses in Mourning" I had no intention at all of 'toppling the gods'. I was merely coming out against the new religion, against those hypocrites who, not without some success, are attempting to convert Marxism into a religion, into a Procrustean bed for science, the arts and love. Sad examples have appeared in the fields of cybernetics and genetics, there are tumultuous flushes of toadstools in literature and art, unending calls for sacrifices and endless promises of a 'future paradise' – is this all not a far cry from the tragedy of Bruno and Galileo, from the writing of psalms and iconography, from monasteries and the Lord's hereafter?

If Marxism is unable to withstand the violent onslaught of dogmatism it is doomed to become a religion. No teaching should monopolize humanity's spiritual life. Even though Einstein made discoveries which shook the foundations of science, he was nevertheless not a political adherent of mine.

16.10.1962

There is nothing more frightening than absolute power in the hands of narrow-minded people.

The head of the collective farm in Yeremenko's[12] village yelled at a meeting in impotence and rage: "I'll give you another 1933!"[13]

Of course, no one even thought of grabbing the ratbag by the collar. And with this single phrase the idiot will destroy the results

---

[12] Mykola Yeremenko, a poet.

[13] Reference to a forced famine in Ukraine in that year (transl.).

of the work of dozens of intelligent people. If our leaders had more sense, brawlers such as these would be gazing up at the sky through iron bars.

21.10.1962

I simply can't stand bureaucratic, patented, satiated wisdom. Whatever quotes dullards might use to prop up their intellectual ceiling, it will still be too low for normal people. Just as space is unfathomable without movement, so poetry is unfathomable without ideas. What kind of space is it if you can't move through it? What kind of poetry is it if it doesn't think? Poetry is beautiful wisdom.

How shallow our humour has become, how squalid our satire has become! Rockers, flea-market traders, tight pants, and trendy haircuts – does this warrant the attention of serious people, wasting words and emotions on such rubbish? And how long have we been grinning at bad literary consultants! I have never even tried to write any deep and meaningful replies to shallow literary works. You can't dive too deeply into a puddle, even if you are a Japanese pearl diver.

I know so little about genetics. The few booklets that I have come across are far too superficial. Who can advise me what to read?

I must write a poem about Herostratus. It would be very apt right now. Earth is teeming with Herostratuses.

09.11.1962

The holidays have ended, and I am ashamed to recall my behaviour yesterday. I acted like a real ratbag, even insulted people. What a pity no one was moved to punch me in the face! I must learn to control myself and wag my tongue a lot less, instead using my brain more.

Belated remorse is always such a pose, but I have no other avenue. I must learn to see myself from the side.

21.06.1963

I haven't opened this notebook for almost half a year, although some of the things, which have transpired these last six months need to be recorded.

I almost became asphyxiated by the powdery smoke of the raging ideological battles. Realism has won yet another victory, not through artistic works, but through administrative measures. In general, I think the danger of formalist insanity was trumped up. At least in Ukraine I haven't come across a single fan of abstractionism or neo-futurism. As always there is the real danger of formalist stupidity in literature. Is this not formalism, when hundreds of half-baked writers suck on a dozen or two so-called eternal ideas according to previously prepared plans: things such as love of labour, respect for parents, love for your neighbour. Formalism begins where ideas end.

If a poet does not produce new ideas and emotions, he becomes a formalist, no matter how much he advertises his so-called allegiance to realism. There can be no grovelling realism. There is the realism which Shevchenko served and then there is the realism which utilizes the services of Dmyterko. These are two different things! The dmyterkos are not the heirs of our long-suffering Literature. They live off it, not for it.

I can hardly be accused of formalism, yet they refrain from printing anything of mine.

06.07.1963

I don't know if everyone has this problem or it's only me. Often doubts destroy any certainty I might have in my fortitude. I have no idea how I will bear up to real trials and tribulations. Will I remain a human being, or will fear blind not only my eyes, but also my brain? This loss of fortitude is a loss of human dignity, which I place above all else. Even above life itself. And yet so many people, intelligent and talented, have saved their life by foregoing their dignity, and turned life into a useless vegetative state. That is the most frightening thing.

The soul craves upheaval, while the intellect fears it.

Last Sunday we were in Odesa where the local blockheads entertained us with their idiotic horror: lest something should happen. In fact, we were forbidden to take the stage at an evening to commemorate Shevchenko. It seems some people are still afraid of Taras [Shevchenko]. Philistines of the revolution.

22.07.1963

I must have started to fade away. In fact, physically I am practically helpless, although morally I am not yet quite exhausted. I feel no fear when I think of death. Perhaps, because it is still far away? It's a strange thing: I don't want to die and yet I have no special thirst for living. These last ten years have been more than enough for me.

Ironically, I look back on my life: soon I will be twenty-nine, but what have I achieved, what have I begun to do that is significant? I haven't lived a proper life, only experiencing a string of petty troubles, petty failures, petty disappointments, and petty successes!

No, I had imagined quite a different life for myself. Those who want very little from life are so lucky – they will never be disappointed by it. The simplest and shortest path to so-called happiness is to become a philistine. A brain capable of giving birth to thoughts is incapable of making its owner happy.

03.09.1963

Summer, brimming with physical and moral exhaustion, is now behind me. Autumn is on the doorstep, and I am looking with hope into its crystal-clear eyes. It has been a meagre, miserly autumn this summer! What can one expect of such a beggar-woman? She is lying just to get a crust of bread.

I spent the whole summer on a deserted island. If it hadn't been for the trip to Kaniv to hear the *Zhaivoronok* (Skylark) choir perform, there would have been nothing to remember it by. In Kaniv I met the artists Alla Horska[14] and H. Zubchenko. I got on especially well with Alla Horska.

My friends are lying low, I haven't heard a word from any of them. The printed media has become even more dull and audacious. The newspaper *Literaturna Ukraina* has castrated my article, the magazine *Ukraina* is making a mockery of my poems. Each lackey does whatever he pleases. How can one fail but to radiate gratefulness, how can one fail not to pray each evening and each morning for those who have given us such freedoms? To this I can add that in April my poems were pulled from *Zmina*, butchered in *Zhovten'* and then I received refusals from the magazines *Dnipro* and *Vitchyzna*.

> Ay, ay, ay, such joy! We're all under the press.
> All this is necessary for our progress.[15]

05.09.1963

Yesterday I wrote *Kazka pro Duryla* (Fairy Tale About Dupe). It was written in one breath, though some parts were penned earlier.

Now I feel even more solitary in Cherkasy, for the collective I worked with at the newspaper *Molod' Cherkashchyny* is no more. My friendship with Nehoda[16] and Ohloblin has cooled irreversibly. I was needed by one of them so long as I could help him, the other turned out to be nothing more than a weathercock. I have no doubt that he will now attack me with the same vigour that he previously praised me. He has in fact already demonstrated this from several

---

[14] Alla Horska (1929-1970), an artist from Kyiv, an active member of the Creative Youth Club. She died under suspicious circumstances, probably at the hands of the KGB.

[15] Poem by Stanislav Telniuk (1935-1990), the full text of which was widely circulated in samizdat form. Only published once in 1966 in Kyiv, but with 16 lines excised.

[16] Mykola Nehoda (1928-2008), a poet, prose writer and author of many songs.

podiums at various meetings. However – we must get on with our own life.

20.09.1963

When I talk of a 'desert island' and my solitude, it has nothing to do with contempt toward other people. The fact that I have hardly any friends in Cherkasy doesn't mean that I consider everyone to be duds, undeserving of my attention, etc. (my wife keeps telling me this). It's just that I haven't been able to find kindred spirits among them, and friendship, of course, cannot survive on rationality alone.

I recently met Bohdan Horyn.

I think my writing has become worse than it was a year ago. My mind and my heart have become lazy.